A FRIENDLY GUIDE TO LUKE'S GOSPEL

Stuart Moran

garratt
PUBLISHING

Published in Australia by
Garratt Publishing
32 Glenvale Crescent
Mulgrave, Vic. 3170

www.garrattpublishing.com.au

Copyright © Stuart Moran 2013

All rights reserved. Except as provided by the Australian copyright law, no part of this book may be reproduced in any way without permission in writing from the publisher.

Design and typesetting by Lynne Muir
Text editing by Juliette Hughes
Images: Susan Daily, pp 3, 4, 12, 16, 21, 22, 24, 26, 28, 33, 39 and Lynne Muir pp 7, 10, 17, 29, 35, 42, 44, 47, 48

Scripture quotations are drawn from the *New Revised Standard Version of the Bible*, copyright © 1989 by the Division of Christian Eduction of the National Council of the Churches of Christ in the USA. Used by permission. All rights reserved.

Nihil Obstat: Reverend Gerard Diamond MA (Oxon), LSS, D.Theol, Diocesan Censor

Imprimatur: Monsignor Greg Bennet, Vicar General

Date: 4 August 2012

The Nihil Obstat and Imprimatur are official declarations that a book or pamphlet is free of doctrinal or moral error. No implication is contained therein that those who have granted the Nihil Obstat and Imprimatur agree with the contents, opinions or statements expressed. They do not necessarily signify that the work is approved as a basic text for catechetical instruction.

9781921946318

Cataloguing in Publication information for this title is available from the National Library of Australia. www.nla.gov.au

The author and publisher gratefully acknowledge the permission granted to reproduce the copyright material in this book. Every effort has been made to trace copyright holders and to obtain their permission for the use of copyright material. The publisher apologises for any errors or omissions in the above list and would be grateful if notified of any corrections that should be incorporated in future reprints or editions of this book.

Garratt Publishing has included on its website a page for special notices in relation to this and our other publications.

Please visit www.garrattpublishing.com.au

Contents

Introduction...3
Luke's Gospel: some basics...............................5
The births of Jesus and of John the Baptist (Luke 1:1-2:52) 9
Baptism, Genealogy and Temptation (Luke 3:1-4:13).................................15
Ministry in Galilee: Divided opinion about Jesus (Luke 4:14-8:56)...............19
Disciples share in Jesus' ministry (Luke 9:1-50)..27
Telling stories on the way to Jerusalem (Luke 9:51-19:44).........................31
Final days in Jerusalem (Luke 19:45-23:56)..38
Resurrection (Luke 24)..43

Luke's 'Must-sees'

- Mary in Luke — 10
- Prayer — 17
- A Gospel for the poor — 21
- A universal message — 24
- God's will and human freedom — 28
- Parables in the travel narrative — 32

Introduction

The Gospel according to Luke tells a story about Jesus of Nazareth, the first century figure whose life, death and resurrection came to form the core of Christianity. Although there are other ancient stories about Jesus (in particular, the Gospels of Matthew, Mark and John), Luke's story is unique. Not only Christianity, but also Western culture generally, would be totally different had Luke's Gospel never been written. Without Luke, we would not have the Annunciation scenes that fill the galleries and churches of Europe. We would not have the cantatas and motets inspired by the texts of Mary's *Magnificat*, Zechariah's *Benedictus* and, of course, the angels' *Gloria in Excelsis Deo*. Newspapers would not refer to unexpected heroes as 'Good Samaritans' and we would not have the parable of the 'Prodigal Son'. We would not know about tree-climbing Zacchaeus or about the 'Good Thief' crucified alongside Jesus.

Most readers of this book have therefore already been exposed to Luke's Gospel in many different ways. Some of you, familiar with the bits of the Gospel that have made their way into Western culture generally, may want to understand something of their original context. For others, your interest in Luke will be related to a Christian faith commitment and you will also be familiar with the Gospel through participation in Christian worship. You may want to refresh your appreciation of Luke's Gospel and perhaps even be surprised by aspects of the Gospel that are a little less familiar.

We are all familiar with travel guidebooks that prepare us for a visit to a foreign country. I think of this *Friendly Guide* in a similar way. Despite our familiarity with Luke's Gospel, there are many aspects of Luke's writing that are totally foreign to us. The Gospel was originally written in another language (a form of ancient Greek), comes to us from the distant past (the first century of the common era 'CE') and from the location and culture of the Roman Empire. We have all met examples of that strange variety of tourist who expects everything to be just the same as at home! But we will get much more out of our visit to the foreign country of Luke's Gospel if we open ourselves to the possibility of being surprised and challenged by what he writes.

As with a travel guidebook, in this book we will get a general overview of the terrain to be covered and then focus on some of the distinctive features and 'must-sees' for our visit there. Of course, our focus will be on Luke's Gospel itself, but the Gospel can't be fully appreciated in isolation. Just as a visit to Italy is enhanced by some understanding of Italy's place in the broader context of European history and culture, so a reading of Luke is enriched by some understanding of the New Testament and the cultural world that produced it. Perhaps you've already read *A Friendly Guide to the New Testament* or something similar. That's a very good way to get a sense of the broader landscape of the New Testament of which Luke's Gospel forms a part. Each and every one of the 27 books of the New Testament is ultimately concerned with Jesus, but each has its own perspective and way of speaking about him. Our exploration of Luke's Gospel will involve seeing what Luke shares in common with other books in the New Testament but also what makes his perspective on Jesus distinctive.

I hope that this book will be interesting and inspiring in its own way, but it's no substitute for actually experiencing Luke's story. If you haven't already done so, try reading the Gospel from beginning to end. For those who are used to hearing Luke in the form of short passages read in the context of church services, the idea of reading the whole Gospel might sound a little daunting. However, it only takes about two hours to read Luke's Gospel – it's no longer than many movies and much shorter than any modern novel.

I also suggest that you try reading the Gospel aloud. The majority of people in Luke's society could not read and were dependent on hearing things read to them. This was also true among the early Christians for whom Luke wrote; he expected them to *hear* rather than read his gospel. Even those who could read in the ancient world tended to read aloud to themselves. Reading the Gospel aloud, either alone or with a group, enables us to appreciate the fact that Luke's words were intended to stimulate the ear as much as the eye. Reading aloud also slows us down slightly; it forces us to give every word and phrase its due and so to resist the temptation to skip over what we think we already know.

Luke's Gospel: some basics – who, when and where?

1Since many have undertaken to set down an orderly account of the events that have been fulfilled among us, 2just as they were handed on to us by those who from the beginning were eyewitnesses and servants of the word, 3I too decided, after investigating everything carefully from the very first, to write an orderly account for you, most excellent Theophilus, 4so that you may know the truth concerning the things about which you have been instructed. (Luke 1:1-4)

Who was Luke?

It is a curious thing that while Luke's Gospel contains the name of the person for whom it was written (Theophilus – 1:3), it doesn't contain the name of its author. In this respect, it is similar to the other three Gospels in the New Testament: all of them are anonymous. The titles we're familiar with – 'the Gospel according to Matthew', 'Mark', 'Luke' or 'John' – are titles that were given to these four writings by early Christians during the second century. That isn't to say that the titles are wrong, but simply to say that they do not form part of the original writings themselves. While it would be interesting to know exactly who composed 'Luke's' Gospel, it adds relatively little to our understanding of the Gospel itself. Nevertheless, it's worth saying a word about the tradition that this Gospel was written by someone called 'Luke', especially since we ourselves know the Gospel by this name. Whatever the historical facts, we can continue to use the name 'Luke' for the author, whoever it actually was.

Later Christian authors thought that the evangelist was the Luke mentioned on a few occasions in the New Testament as a companion of Paul (Philemon 24; Col 4:14; 2 Tim 4:11). Both Luke's Gospel and the Acts of the Apostles appear to have been written by the same person, a person who at various points in Acts also appears to have been travelling around with Paul (Acts 16:10-17; 20:5-15; 21:1-18; 27:1-28:16).

Some things can be gleaned from the Gospel itself about its author. In the first place, he is clearly a cultivated and highly literate person; the style of Greek he uses is polished. Greek was the international language of the Roman Empire (much like English is for us today) and Luke was probably a native speaker of Greek. Luke's frequent allusions to the Old Testament suggest to some that he may have come from a Jewish background, but he is also particularly interested in the fact that the Good News of Jesus is not only for Jews but also for non-Jews ('Gentiles'). He also makes occasional mistakes about Jewish rituals that are difficult to explain if he had grown up as a Jew.

For these reasons, many experts think that Luke came from a non-Jewish background, but had been immersed in the ancient Greek translation of the Hebrew scriptures (our 'Old Testament'), perhaps in preparation for conversion to Judaism. At some point, though, he was exposed to preaching about Jesus of Nazareth as the long-awaited Jewish Messiah and became a believer in Jesus. Given his reliance on 'eyewitnesses' (1:2), it is unlikely that he himself had known Jesus during his earthly life.

Where and when was Luke's Gospel written?

If identifying the author of the Gospel is difficult, it's even more challenging to pinpoint where and when the Gospel was written. Again, this is not of critical importance for our understanding of the Gospel.

> GIVEN HIS RELIANCE ON 'EYEWITNESSES' (1:2), IT IS UNLIKELY THAT [LUKE] HIMSELF HAD KNOWN JESUS DURING HIS EARTHLY LIFE.

Experts estimate the date of the writing of Luke's Gospel and the Acts to the year 80CE or slightly later. We can well imagine that a young man in his twenties or thirties who was involved in Paul's missionary activity in the early 50s CE could still be writing, now with the benefit of many years of reflection, in the 80s. All we can be certain about is that the Gospel was written somewhere in the eastern part of the Roman Empire between Greece and Syria towards the end of the first century.

That may not sound like much, but even to say that much should remind us that the Gospel comes to us from a time and place which is almost unimaginably different from our own. And it's for that very reason that we need some kind of guide if we are not to distort Luke's work by imposing our own cultural assumptions on it.

> THE GOSPEL COMES TO US FROM A TIME AND PLACE WHICH IS ALMOST UNIMAGINABLY DIFFERENT FROM OUR OWN.

What exactly is Luke's Gospel?

What kind of writing is this book we call 'Luke's Gospel'? The answer might seem to be obvious: a gospel! But that answer only forces us to ask what a 'gospel' is. At its simplest, a gospel has come to be recognised as a story about Jesus of Nazareth which tells how his public ministry of preaching, miraculous works and teaching of disciples ended in his execution by the authorities in Jerusalem and his being raised from the dead on the third day. The Gospels of Matthew, Mark and John are other examples of such stories about Jesus.

Most experts today think that Mark's Gospel is the oldest of the four gospels in the New Testament (the order of the books in our printed Bibles is not necessarily the order of their composition). In fact, we could say that Mark invented the idea of a gospel and provided a model or template for both Matthew and Luke to follow (John's Gospel is quite different from these three). Certainly, a very great deal of Mark's Gospel is repeated, either directly or with some modification, in Luke's Gospel. Of course, as we shall see, Luke himself adds a lot of material to Mark's basic story.

It's important to take seriously the fact that the Gospels, including Luke's, are in the form of a *story*. The New Testament and other early Christian literature provide many examples of other kinds of writing about Jesus: letters, hymns, prayers, visions, theological statements and prophecies, to name a few. In other words, of all the different kinds of writing that Luke could have chosen to write about Jesus, he chose the form of a story. Luke seems to be particularly conscious of his choice since right at the outset he says that he is following in the footsteps of others who have written 'orderly accounts' or 'narratives' about Jesus (1:1).

The fact that Luke chose to write about Jesus in the form of a story is one of the reasons why it is important to read the entire gospel from beginning to end. A story is inherently dramatic – it is not just a list of events, but a carefully crafted ordering of events that builds and resolves tension. To put it simply: a story contains a plot. As we shall see, for Luke the plot of the story concerns God's visitation of his chosen people Israel through the person of his Son and Messiah. The drama revolves around the question of whether or not God's people will recognise and accept this visitation. There is a surprising twist in the story, as it begins to appear that Gentiles (non-Jews) will more readily accept Israel's Messiah than Israel itself.

Stories, of course, can be fictional or non-fictional. Luke tells his audience right at the beginning that he is not writing fiction, but 'an orderly account of the events that have been fulfilled among us' (1:1). This sounds to us as though Luke is writing that particular kind of non-fiction that we call history, and it is fair to say that Luke was the Christian community's first 'historian'. We need to be a little careful here though, since Luke also tells his audience that he is writing with a particular aim in mind.

In other words, Luke understands his job as not just to give facts but also to interpret them in a way that supports and strengthens faith in Jesus; and to do that not simply as an historical figure, but as the crucified and risen Messiah who is sent by God and through whose name alone human beings can be saved. Although it is certainly possible to gain information from the gospel about the man Jesus of Nazareth who lived in Galilee and Judea in the early first century, providing that information for its own sake is not Luke's intention.

I mentioned earlier that Luke's Gospel and the Acts of the Apostles appear to have the same author and in fact seem to be two volumes of a single story. Both books are addressed by name to Theophilus (Luke 1:3; Acts 1:1), and the beginning of Acts refers explicitly to 'the first book' with a description that clearly matches Luke's Gospel. The two books deal with two different periods of time: the Gospel deals with the earthly ministry of Jesus up to and including his death, resurrection and ascension, while the Acts deals with the ministry of the early Church in the name of the Risen Jesus up until the time Paul is imprisoned in Rome. That said, the two books were probably intended by Luke to be read together as a continuous story. Many of the questions that the Gospel sets up are never answered within the Gospel, but only in the Acts. In particular, the idea that Jesus will be a 'light for revelation to the Gentiles' (Luke 1:1) seems to remain unfulfilled until the early Christians (who of course were mainly of

Jewish background) begin to evangelise Gentiles, not only within the Holy Land but throughout the Empire – a story only told in Acts.

Why did Luke write his gospel?

So why does Luke write his Gospel? Luke himself admits that he knows other people have written accounts about 'the things that have been fulfilled amongst us' (1:1). What made him think that the story of Jesus that he knew from Mark's Gospel needed to be re-told? For one thing, Luke's investigations have brought him into contact with stories and traditions about what Jesus said and did that Mark did not include in his Gospel. Luke has expanded Mark's basic story with such things as an account of Jesus' birth, with many parables, with longer sections of Jesus' teaching and with a detailed account of what occurs around his death and resurrection. Luke also seems to sense that Mark's story is unfinished in the sense that any story about the life of Jesus must include an account of how the Risen Jesus continues to work powerfully in the world through the Spirit-filled community of believers. This at least partly explains the need for the Acts of the Apostles as a second volume of Luke's work.

Luke's reasons for writing go beyond a need to 'fill out' Mark's story. Fortunately for us, Luke himself explains why he is writing right at the beginning of his Gospel. Addressing Theophilus, Luke says he is writing so that 'you may know the truth concerning the things about which you have been instructed' (1:4). Theophilus has already been 'instructed' – perhaps he is a newly baptised Christian, or at least someone who is preparing for baptism. While Luke is certainly interested in conveying the truth for Theophilus' benefit, he is not just reciting facts or adding information, but telling a story which links events together in a way that assures Theophilus (and his other readers, including us) that God is in control of what happens in this story at every step of the way. The words 'know the truth' can also be translated as 'have certainty' or 'be assured'. But why does Theophilus need re-assurance?

Luke has a particular interest in the fact that the Good News about Jesus is for all people. We tend to take for granted that God 'shows no partiality, but in every nation anyone who fears him and does what is

Luke's Gospel: some basics 7

right is acceptable to him' (Acts 10:34). But this would have been a surprising statement for most people in the ancient world.

The God of Israel had shown himself in the scriptures of Israel to be particularly partial to one people that he himself had chosen to be his own. In fact, Luke's Gospel demonstrates God's special treatment of his Chosen People; from Luke's point of view, in Jesus, the God of Israel has visited his people *in person*.

However, as the story of the Gospel unfolds, it becomes clear that not everyone in Israel will recognise this. What may be causing problems for an intelligent Gentile like Theophilus is trying to understand why this happened. Did God's plans go wrong? Did God treat his own people fairly? Can God really be trusted?

In order to reassure Theophilus, Luke's Gospel tells a story of the God of Israel keeping faith with his Chosen People, while opening up the possibility of a relationship between God and the Gentiles. One of the problems that the early Christians faced was to explain why the vast majority of the Jewish people had rejected their own Messiah. At one level, the explanation for this was simple: the idea that God's Messiah could have been executed as a criminal by the Romans was outrageously unacceptable. No Jew expected the Messiah to be put to death.

Those who did come to accept that Jesus was the Messiah also came to the conclusion that he had both gone to his death and been raised from the dead in accordance with God's plan. But this raised another question: had God really acted fairly towards his own special people, Israel, in doing something so unexpected? And if God had not acted fairly with his own people, how could Gentiles possibly put their trust in him?

Luke tries to answer these questions in different ways. In his Gospel, he shows that the Messiah is a prophetic figure who shares in the suffering and rejection that so often marked the people of Israel's treatment of the prophets sent to them by God. In the Acts of the Apostles, he recounts through the preaching of Peter that the scriptures of Israel did in fact prepare for a suffering Messiah, and that God had therefore acted justly. The theme of God's faithfulness towards his people is prominent right at the outset of the Gospel. The announcement of the birth of John – who will 'turn many of the people of Israel to the Lord their God' and 'make ready a people prepared for the Lord' – occurs in the very heart of the nation (the Jerusalem Temple) and involves a couple who are outstanding representatives of their people in terms of being 'righteous before God'.

This indicates clearly that the God of the Old Testament is the very same God who will in fact be the principal character in Luke's Gospel. The gospel will also end in the Jerusalem Temple (24:52), from where the 'forgiveness of sins is to be proclaimed ... to all nations' – for the people of Israel are God's special, but not sole, concern. As the story of the Acts progresses we see the Good News being proclaimed in ever-widening circles. The second volume of Luke's story will end in Rome, the heart of the Empire, symbolising the universal reach of the Good News. Not only Theophilus, but also the vast majority of Christians today who are not of Jewish background, can see in Luke's two-volume work the beginnings of their own story.

Did you know?

- That in the New Testament non-Jews are often called 'Gentiles'?
- That the name Theophilus means 'Friend of God'?
- That Luke's Gospel and the Acts of the Apostles are two volumes of a single story?
- That Luke uses Mark's Gospel as a model?

The births of Jesus and John the Baptist (Luke 1:1-2:52)

Beginning the Journey

Of the four evangelists, only Luke and Matthew show any interest in Jesus' birth and early childhood. We owe all the familiar elements of our Christmas Nativity scenes to Matthew and Luke. These scenes tend to blend the two stories together, but while the two Gospels share some things in common, in fact they tell the story of Jesus' birth from quite different angles. Matthew tells the story from the perspective of Joseph, while Luke's version is told from Mary's point of view. Matthew tells us about an annunciation to Joseph, the murderous plots of King Herod, the visit of the wise men from the east, and the flight into Egypt. Luke mentions none of this, but instead gives us the annunciation to Mary, the journey to Bethlehem, angel choirs and shepherds, and the fact that the newborn child is placed in a manger. Luke is also unique in intertwining the story of Jesus' origins with those of John the Baptist. Here, we want to try to understand Luke's story without unnecessary interference from Matthew.

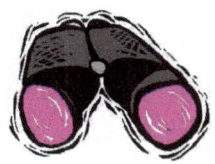

Luke's Gospel begins with the foretelling of John's birth (1:5-25). Luke sets out to create an old-fashioned atmosphere for this part of the story. He begins 'in the days of King Herod of Judea', which for the people who first heard Luke's Gospel were already in the distant past (Herod had been dead for around a century). The first two characters introduced to us are also representatives of a lost world: Zechariah, a priest of the Jerusalem Temple, and his wife Elizabeth.

By Luke's time, the Temple lay in ruins after its brutal destruction by the Romans in 70CE. Zechariah and Elizabeth could easily have stepped from the pages of the Old Testament as models of genuine Israelite piety and devotion. There is a problem, however: they are childless. In a society that understood fertility as a divine blessing, Elizabeth represents a paradox: a pious woman who has not been blessed with children. For her, her childlessness is worse than disappointing – it is a 'disgrace' (1:25). There is a delightful play on this theme since the name of her child, John, comes from the Hebrew for 'mercy or grace of God'.

After the annunciation of John's birth to his father, Zechariah, Luke jumps forward six months and shifts the scene dramatically away from the heart of the Jewish nation to the tiny village of Nazareth in distant Galilee. Now there is an annunciation of the birth of another child, Jesus, to his mother Mary. This sets the pattern for the whole of the first two chapters of the Gospel where the story switches back and forth between that of John and that of Jesus. Despite the parallels between the two children, though, Luke is careful to show that Jesus is the more important of the two.

It's clear, for example, that Luke understands John to be the result of ordinary sexual relations between Zechariah and Elizabeth, even if that conception has been in some way divinely assisted; this is in accordance with a number of Old Testament stories in which couples thought to be infertile are granted a child in answer to prayer, such as Samson (Judges 13:1-25) and Samuel (1 Sam 1:1-20). In contrast, the birth of Jesus is altogether unprecedented; this child has no human father, but is conceived in Mary's womb by the Holy Spirit's power. While John will be 'great in the sight of the Lord' (1:15), Jesus will be both 'great' *and* 'will be called Son of the Most High' (1:32). The two annunciation scenes have a lot in common.

> THE VISITATION OF AN ANGEL IS USUALLY A PROFOUNDLY UPSETTING EXPERIENCE; ZECHARIAH IS TERRIFIED, AND MARY IS DEEPLY TROUBLED – THESE ARE APPROPRIATE RESPONSES TO THE CLOSENESS OF GOD'S PRESENCE.

Mary in Luke

Mark's Gospel hardly ever mentions Mary the mother of Jesus. Mark mentions her by name only once, as he reports the mildly insulting way the villagers of Nazareth dismiss Jesus as unimportant: 'the carpenter, the son of Mary' (Mark 6:8). Elsewhere, Mark refers to her simply as 'his [Jesus'] mother' (Mark 3:31-34).

For Luke, Mary is a much more significant character. Luke mentions her more frequently, especially in the stories surrounding the birth and childhood of Jesus. Luke also presents Mary in a more positive light than Mark. The angel Gabriel calls her 'favoured one' and states that the Lord is with her. Elizabeth calls Mary 'blessed … among women'. No one else in Luke's story gets such a ringing endorsement!

Luke does keep Jesus' statement that is found also in Mark's gospel: 'My mother and my brothers are those who hear the word of God and do it' (8:21). But in Luke's Gospel this can hardly be understood as denigrating Mary, since Luke has already shown that she is the model of someone who hears God's word and responds by putting it into practice: 'Here am I, the servant of the Lord; let it be with me according to your word' (1:38). Mary is most truly in intimate relationship with Jesus, not because she is his physical mother, but because she responds appropriately to the divine word. It is through hearing and doing God's word, announced by the angel, that she becomes the mother of Jesus in the first place.

Mary's obedience is not blind. She is characterised by Luke as a true daughter of Israel who places her trust in God because she knows her people have experienced God's faithfulness to them over centuries. Nevertheless, she asks questions about what is not clear to her: 'how can this come about, since I am a virgin?' (Luke 1:34). Mary is portrayed as both thoughtful and prayerful on more than one occasion. In the Acts of the Apostles, Luke names Mary as being one of those 'constantly devoting themselves to prayer' with the apostles (Acts 1:14).

Luke's presentation of Mary is part of a developing interest in the mother of Jesus' that can be traced in the New Testament.

Paul, whose letters are among the earliest writings in the New Testament, shows no interest in Mary as a character in her own right: only in passing does Paul refer to Jesus as being 'born of a woman' (Gal 4:4). Mark, the first of the gospels, makes some bare biographical references to the family of Jesus including Mary. Luke, as we have seen, is somewhat interested in the events in which Mary takes part, but is also beginning to portray her as a figure of ideal discipleship. By the time of the writing of John's Gospel, perhaps twenty years after Luke, Mary is less important as an individual figure than as a symbolic or representative one.

Angels and Announcements

The same angel, Gabriel, is sent to both Zechariah and to Mary. Gabriel's name in Hebrew means 'my strength is God', suggesting a particularly imposing or overwhelming presence. In the Bible, angels are not comforting, gentle creatures! The visitation of an angel is usually a profoundly upsetting experience; Zechariah is terrified, and Mary is deeply troubled – these are appropriate responses to the closeness of the divine presence. Nevertheless, Gabriel tells them not to be afraid and assures them that they are recipients of special divine favour. Natural terror must be replaced with a holy awe if they are to hear and understand the message.

Despite these common themes, one of the major differences between the annunciation stories is the uneven treatment meted out to Zechariah and to Mary when they question Gabriel about the announcements the angel has just made to each. Zechariah asks, 'How will I know that this is so? For I am an old man and my wife is getting on in years' (1:18) and his question earns him a period of nine months' inability to speak. Mary asks, 'How can this be, since I am a virgin?' (1:34) and appears to suffer no consequences.

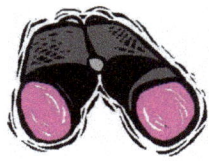

Why is Zechariah punished while Mary is not? Is God really that capricious? In fact, there is a key difference between the questions that they ask. By asking how he can know for sure that what the angel has announced will come true, Zechariah questions the believability of the angel's message and thus casts doubt on the truthfulness of God's speech. Zechariah's question indicates a fundamental lack of faith since he seeks a 'better' way of knowing. The angel's point is that if God says something will be so, God's speech is its own guarantee. On the other hand, Mary does not seek any further proof about what is to happen; she simply asks 'how' it will occur in the face of the fact that she is still a virgin.

There is delicious irony in the fact that the experienced priest in the Jerusalem Temple botches his encounter with God, while a teenage girl in an obscure village demonstrates exactly the right attitude. Luke delights in the fact that those on the margins are shown to be God's favourites. Indeed, this is the theme of Mary's song, the Magnificat (1:46-55).

46 And Mary said,
'My soul magnifies the Lord, 47 and my spirit rejoices in God my Saviour, 48 for he has looked with favour on the lowliness of his servant. Surely, from now on all generations will call me blessed; 49 for the Mighty One has done great things for me, and holy is his name. 50 His mercy is for those who fear him from generation to generation. 51 He has shown strength with his arm; he has scattered the proud in the thoughts of their hearts. 52 He has brought down the powerful from their thrones, and lifted up the lowly; 53 he has filled the hungry with good things, and sent the rich away empty. 54 He has helped his servant Israel, in remembrance of his mercy,
55 according to the promise he made to our ancestors, to Abraham and to his descendants for ever.' (Lk 1:46-55)

Mary is introduced to us as being engaged to a man named Joseph (1:27), but Joseph plays very little part in Luke's story. Joseph's significance is simply that he is a descendant of King David and it is through his marriage to Mary that Jesus too can be considered a descendant of David. David himself lived in the 10th century BCE and was the founder of a dynasty that lasted until the destruction of Jerusalem and exile of its inhabitants to Babylon in the early 6th century BCE. At that time the Davidic monarchy came to an end.

It is important to realise that King Herod and his family were not descendants of David but fortune hunters who had been set in place as puppet kings by Rome. By the time of Jesus, many Jews expected that the Messiah would be a descendant of David who would liberate the land of Israel from the Romans and re-establish the ancient monarchy. Thus the fact that Jesus is legally Joseph's son is important for Luke's claim that Jesus is the Messiah. We shall return to what it might mean for Jesus to

> IT HAS BEEN SUGGESTED THAT THE FIRST TWO CHAPTERS OF LUKE'S GOSPEL ARE A BIT LIKE A MUSICAL, WITH THE ACTION AND DIALOGUE CONSTANTLY BEING INTERRUPTED BY CHARACTERS BURSTING INTO SONG!

be 'Messiah' when we look at the beginning of his public ministry in Galilee.

The two stories of John and Jesus meet in the scene usually called The Visitation of Mary to Elizabeth (1:39-56). The link between the stories is made by telling us that the two women are relatives (1:36). Elizabeth is the first human character in the Gospel to recognise the coming of the Messiah. Once again, this ties in to Luke's desire to show God's fidelity to Israel. In a way, Elizabeth symbolically represents her whole people as she recognises what God is doing in Mary's life – something similar will occur with Simeon and Anna after the actual birth of Jesus (2:22-38). Elizabeth is filled with the Holy Spirit – a sure sign that she is about to prophesy, that is, to speak on God's behalf. Later in the birth stories, Zechariah and Simeon will also be filled with the Holy Spirit before speaking. Like Gabriel, Elizabeth extols Mary's blessedness that she links to Mary's ready willingness to believe (unlike her own husband, Zechariah) 'that there would be a fulfilment of what was spoken to her by the Lord' (1:45).

At this point Mary begins a speech in praise of God (1:46-55), usually called the *Magnificat* from its initial word in the Latin translation. The lyrical quality of these verses has led to the *Magnificat* traditionally being called a song or canticle. Even if Mary did not sing these words, composers through the centuries have set them to music. This is in fact the first of four canticles in Luke's birth stories; the others are Zechariah's *Benedictus* following the naming of John (1:68-79), the angels' chorus *Gloria in Excelsis Deo* following the birth of Jesus (2:14), and Simeon's *Nunc dimittis* (2:29-32). It has been suggested that the first two chapters of Luke's Gospel are a bit like a musical, with the action and dialogue constantly being interrupted by characters bursting into song! Like songs in a musical, these canticles provide a kind of interpretation of the action; in particular, they make it clear that everything that is going on with the birth of John and Jesus is in accordance with God's plan.

12 FRIENDLY GUIDE TO LUKE'S GOSPEL

That Mary is 'blessed' is entirely due to the undeserved action of God on her behalf – it is her very lowliness that attracts God's eyes (1:48), for God has always acted preferentially on behalf of the poor and the powerless. That a young girl from a little village should be chosen to be mother of the Messiah fits into a pattern evident from the Old Testament; this is the way God always acts! In particular, Luke probably expects his readers to remember that King David himself was the youngest and least qualified of his brothers to be chosen as king (1 Sam 16:1-13). Likewise, David's descendant will come from origins that, by human standards, seem unlikely.

NAMING JOHN

After Mary's return home, the story focuses again on John. John's birth is described quite simply. The little controversy over the naming of the child is touchingly personal with the extended family all weighing-in on the matter and threatening to take control (1:59-62). But they cannot be allowed to frustrate God's plans. Finally, Zechariah is brought back into the picture as he is asked what he wants the child called. There is another touch of ironic humour here: it is Zechariah himself, who doubted the truth of Gabriel's words ('Your wife Elizabeth will bear you a son, *and you will name him John*'), and who must bring about their final fulfilment by naming the child! After nine months of enforced silence, it's no wonder that words come tumbling forth from Zechariah's mouth as he launches into his great canticle of praise, the Benedictus (1:67-79).

Curiously, the *Benedictus* begins with praising God for raising up 'a mighty saviour for us in the house of David his servant' (1:69) even though Jesus has not yet been born; only then does Zechariah praise God for the birth of his own son, John who will be a 'prophet of the Most High' (1:76). As Elizabeth did, Zechariah recognises that Jesus will be the greater of these two children. After the *Benedictus* we are told no more about John except that he becomes 'strong in spirit' and 'was in the wilderness', motifs that remind us of John's prophetic identity and prepare us for the account of his ministry beginning in chapter three.

JESUS ON THE MOVE

The story of the birth of Jesus begins with a reference to the census ordered by Augustus, the first Roman emperor (2:1-3). Historically, it is difficult to identify an empire-wide census being taken at the time of Jesus' birth, but Luke's aim here is not to teach us history. Rather, Luke reminds us of the wider world in which this drama is being played out, the world of the Roman Empire. As his story progresses, we will see more and more hints that the birth of the Messiah will have implications not only for the Jewish people, but also for the whole world. In Luke's story the census also provides a reason for Joseph and Mary to travel to Bethlehem, the hometown of King David and thus reinforces the claim that Jesus is the Messiah.

Given that Luke usually wants to show that Jesus is more important than John, the actual circumstances of their births are strangely reversed. While Elizabeth enjoyed the support of her kinswoman Mary's presence leading up to the birth of John, Mary herself seems to enjoy no such support. While John is born at home and into the loving and secure embrace of family and neighbours (1:57-66), Jesus is born far from home, amongst strangers, and laid in a feed trough for animals (2:4-7). Luke's reference to a manger probably led to the tradition that Jesus' birth took place in a stable even though neither Matthew nor Luke refers to one. Despite the humble circumstances of his birth, Jesus' pre-eminence is quickly re-established. While Elizabeth's immediate circle of 'neighbours and relatives' rejoices at the birth of John, the birth of Jesus is accompanied by angels proclaiming that his birth will mean 'great joy for all the people' (2:10). For the first time in the Gospel, Jesus is proclaimed as the 'Christ', the Messiah. This proclamation is not made to the rich and powerful but to shepherds – people amongst the lowest strata of ancient society who receive the news joyfully and respond 'with haste'.

> THE ADVENT OF THE MESSIAH, WHICH UNTIL NOW HAS BEEN PORTRAYED AND GREETED IN ALMOST ENTIRELY POSITIVE TERMS FOR ISRAEL, WILL IN FACT BRING ABOUT DIVISION IN ISRAEL ITSELF: SOME RISE AND OTHERS FALL.

The final two episodes in the birth stories, traditionally called the Presentation in the Temple and the Finding in the Temple, form the climax of the opening part of Luke's Gospel (2:22-52). In both stories, Jesus is depicted as growing up in a traditionally pious Jewish environment. To the casual observer, Jesus is a perfectly ordinary little Jewish boy. But as Mary and Joseph do what is required of them by the Law, new characters, Simeon and Anna, unexpectedly appear and begin to speak in prophetic language about the child. This child is no ordinary Israelite but the sign of God's salvation and not only for Israel but also for Gentiles. Amidst the joyful proclamation there are warnings: the child will be a cause of division in Israel, division whose effects will touch even his mother. Simeon and Anna thus not only confirm what has been promised already about Jesus, but also point to new developments in the story.

The final canticle of the birth stories, the *Nunc dimittis*, is pronounced by Simeon (2:29-32). The canticle emphasises that Jesus represents the fulfilment of ancient hopes for salvation and thus God's fidelity to his people ('glory to your people Israel'). However, in the very heart of Judaism, the Temple, Simeon also pronounces good news for non-Jews ('a light for revelation to the Gentiles'). Nothing in the Gospel so far has prepared us for this idea of 'universal' salvation. The annunciation to Mary characterised the child to be born as the restored Davidic king reigning 'over the house of Jacob'. The angelic chorus announced that a Saviour had been born, but there was still no reference to non-Israelites. The good news of great joy for 'all the people' sounds in English as if it referred to everyone, but the Greek word Luke uses here refers to *the people of Israel* rather than *the peoples* in general. Even Mary is 'amazed' (2:33) – this is not expected, even by the one character in the story so far who, better than anyone, knows the identity of her son.

As if this were not enough, Simeon goes further. The advent of the Messiah has been portrayed as an essentially positive event for Israel, but now we read that it shall be divisive: some rise and others fall. Mary herself acknowledged in her *Magnificat* that God's mighty work exalts some and humbles others, but until now it could not have been predicted that this would apply to Israel itself. After all the rejoicing of the birth stories, Simeon's canticle is thus the first real omen that the story to follow will be a story of conflict.

VISITING THE TEMPLE

Simeon does not only speak of conflict for Israel, but also of a 'sword' that will pierce Mary's soul. What this will mean will be developed further on in the Gospel, but even at this point Luke tells a story of a childhood incident which leaves Mary feeling wounded and confused by the behavior of her son (2:41-52). The plot of this little story is clear enough: a journey home to Nazareth after a Passover pilgrimage to Jerusalem is interrupted when the child Jesus goes missing. After a frantic search, the child is found in unexpected circumstances—not distressed and disoriented at having been left behind by his parents—but in the midst of debate about the Jewish Law (or Torah) in the Temple precincts. Challenged by his parents, Jesus claims not to be 'lost' at all, but to be more fully at home in the environs of the Temple where he can be about 'the affairs of his Father'.

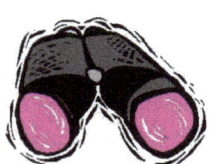

The story of the Finding in the Temple is Luke's first opportunity to develop the idea that the child to be born to Mary would be called Son of God (1:35). It is worth noting that in this little story, neither Mary nor Joseph are ever named but are simply called 'his parents'. In fact, the story is full of words like 'parent' (2:41,43), 'father' (2:48,49), and 'mother' (2:48,51). Luke plays on the ambiguity of these terms to create ironic confusion: the child appears to have abandoned his father and mother, and yet expresses surprise at their frantic searching for him as he claims to have been 'in his Father's things' all the while.

As they were amazed at Simeon's words, so his parents are astounded again (2:48). In Mary's case, however, astonishment gives way to treasuring all these things in her heart: that is, to contemplation (2:51). Jesus is a sign that continues to require interpretation, even by faithful Israel and even by his own mother. Mary's contemplative response is a fitting conclusion to the birth stories. These stories leave many questions waiting to be answered, and Mary's contemplation encourages us to read on.

Did you know?

- That the Christmas Nativity scenes are a combination of the stories in Matthew's and Luke's Gospels?
- That Luke's story shows how God chooses those who are unimportant in the world's eyes to carry out his plans?
- That Luke tells the story of Jesus' annunciation and birth from Mary's point of view?

Baptism, Genealogy and Temptation
(Luke 3:1-4:13)

Between the end of chapter two and the beginning of chapter three there is a great gap in time. The world has changed in the meantime: the rule of two of the longest-reigning monarchs in the ancient world (King Herod the Great and the Emperor Augustus) has come to an end. There is a new Emperor, Tiberius, and Herod's kingdom of Judea has been split up among his sons, one of whom is also called Herod (3:1). We were told that Jesus was twelve years old at the time of the finding in the Temple (2:41) and that he was about thirty years old when he began his public ministry (3:23). That Luke can simply leap over most of Jesus' childhood and young adulthood without comment shows how different the Gospel is from any ordinary biography. A modern historian would be interested to know, for example, whether Jesus learnt to read and write, whether he showed other signs of precocious ability, and whether he learnt Joseph's trade.

Luke's first interest is in developing the startling claim, already made in the birth stories, that Jesus will be called Son of God. It is no coincidence that the last thing we hear about Jesus' childhood includes the first words we hear him speak, an acknowledgement on his part that God is his Father: 'Did you not know that I must be in my Father's house?' (2:49). Luke's account of the baptism, genealogy, and temptation of Jesus will confirm not only that Jesus is God's Son, but also test what that could mean (3:1-4:13).

The beginning of this part of the Gospel is strangely anti-climactic (3:1-6). With great solemnity, Luke lists the names of emperor, governor, kings and high priests; but the word of God does not come to any of these important people. Instead, it comes to John: an unknown, isolated prophet in the desert of a backwater province of the empire. Once again we see Luke's love of God's topsy-turvy way of doing things: 'he has brought down the powerful from their thrones, and lifted up the lowly'.

John the Baptist does indeed 'prepare the way of the Lord' by performing, in miniature, a kind of ministry that serves as an example for that of Jesus. As with the birth stories, John's ministry will be paralleled and then surpassed by that of Jesus, as John himself acknowledges: 'I baptize you with water … He will baptize you with the Holy Spirit and fire' (3:16). John preaches repentance and proclaims good news. He talks specifically to tax collectors and soldiers, not to condemn them, but to show how they need not find themselves excluded from the 'salvation of God' if they do their jobs honestly and justly (3:10-14).

Many of John's hearers would have found this surprising, since tax collectors and soldiers were effectively collaborators with the Roman occupation of the Holy Land. John's association with such people on the margins of what was considered 'holy' prepares us to see Jesus doing the same thing. Luke's Gospel is particularly rich in stories about encounters between Jesus and tax collectors; it is only in Luke, for example, that we find the lovely story of the tax collector Zacchaeus, who is shunned by his neighbours and unexpectedly becomes Jesus' host (19:1-10).

> 21 Now when all the people were baptized, and when Jesus also had been baptized and was praying, the heaven was opened, 22and the Holy Spirit descended upon him in bodily form like a dove. And a voice came from

---

JOHN EMBODIES SO MANY MESSIANIC CHARACTERISTICS THAT MANY IN THE CROWDS MISTAKE HIM FOR THE MESSIAH, RATHER THAN THE MESSIAH'S FORERUNNER. THEY CAN HARDLY BE BLAMED, SINCE IN CONTRAST TO JOHN'S DRAMATIC MINISTRY, THE ADULT JESUS ENTERS THE SCENE IN A VERY UNDERSTATED WAY.

heaven, 'You are my Son, the Beloved; with you I am well pleased.' (Luke 3: 21-22)

John embodies so many Messianic characteristics that many in the crowds mistake him for the Messiah, rather than the Messiah's forerunner. They can hardly be blamed, since in contrast to John's dramatic ministry, the adult Jesus enters the scene in a very understated way. His baptism itself is not actually described (contrast Mark 1:9-10). We are simply told that after he had been baptised, during an experience of prayer, he was addressed by a heavenly voice as 'my Son, the beloved' (3:22). Following this revelation, Luke provides us with a genealogy or family tree (3:23-38).

It's interesting to compare Luke's genealogy with the quite different version in Matthew's Gospel (Matt 1:1-17). Matthew traces Jesus' descent from Abraham, while Luke goes in the opposite direction, describing each generation as 'son of', so that the word 'son' continues to ring in our ears from the baptism scene. Luke's genealogy stretches back beyond Abraham all the way to Adam, who himself is described as 'son of God'. While Matthew's genealogy stresses Jesus' Jewishness as a child of Abraham, Luke's version relates Jesus to *all* human beings through Adam and implies that, since all human beings are 'sons of Adam', so all are children of God.

SOJOURN IN THE DESERT

The same Holy Spirit that descended upon Jesus after his baptism now leads the Son of God into the wilderness or desert (4:1). We already know of the Spirit's role in the birth of Jesus (1:18-20) and that Jesus will baptise with the Spirit, a promise which will not actually be fulfilled until the account of Pentecost in Acts 2:1-4. Jesus' time in the desert is clearly portrayed as something divinely ordained and thus sets the context for the satanic temptations to come: the reader knows that Jesus has been accompanied to this place by the Spirit. The desert is not a place that belongs to the devil but a place where the Spirit may lead.

The desert is a key place in the biblical imagination. Above all, it recalls the place of preparation of the people of Israel for their eventual entry to the Promised Land. The reference to forty days strengthens the impression that we should compare Jesus' time of testing with that of the Israelites' forty years in the wilderness (Exod 16:35; Num 32:13). Unlike the Israelites, who frequently prove themselves unfaithful in this time, Jesus will demonstrate complete fidelity to God's will during his time in the wilderness.

While we usually think of this passage as the 'temptations in the desert', the word 'to tempt' can also have the sense of 'to try,' 'to test' or 'to prove.' This is implied by the devil's own questioning: '*if* you are the Son of God' (4:3,9). In parts of the Old Testament such as the book of Job, the devil (or 'Satan') plays exactly this role as a kind

PRAYER

Luke's account of the baptism of Jesus makes some small but significant changes to Mark's story. One of these is Luke's mention of the fact that the descent of the Holy Spirit occurred while Jesus was praying after his baptism (compare Luke 3:21-22 with Mark 1:9-11). In fact, a close look at Luke's Gospel shows that Luke often adds references to prayer in the episodes he takes over from Mark. For example, in Luke – but not Mark – the important events of the Transfiguration (9:28), the choosing of the Twelve (6:12), and asking the Twelve 'who do you say I am?' (9:18), all take place while Jesus is said to be at prayer.

At all these key moments Jesus is shown explicitly to be in prayerful communion with his Father. God is thus brought into direct contact with the story at these important points and we are again reminded that it is God's will that is the underlying driving force in this story. Naturally, Luke also repeats references to prayer that he finds in Mark. In addition, Luke alone recounts a parable of Jesus 'about the need to pray always and not to lose heart': the parable of the widow and the unjust judge (18:1-8), which he follows with another unique parable about acceptable prayer: the parable of the Pharisee and the tax collector in the Temple (18:9-14). Prayer has a particular importance for Luke's story.

We should also notice that the gospel itself begins in an atmosphere of prayer: 'Now at the time of the incense offering, the whole assembly of the people was praying outside' (1:10). So too at the beginning of Acts, the assembly of the disciples are gathered in prayer together with Mary (Acts 1:14) in preparation for further revelation from God regarding the next stage in the unfolding of his plan. In Acts, in particular, the teaching and example of Jesus' prayer will bear fruit. Daily prayer is a part of the community's life: 'They devoted themselves to the apostles' teaching and fellowship, to the breaking of bread and the prayers' (Acts 2:42). Almost no significant step in the early Church's life occurs without prayer.

Luke's portrayal of Jesus as a person habitually in prayerful communion with God reinforces the identity of Jesus as the Son. When Luke lets us in on the content of Jesus' prayer, we find that it is addressed to God precisely as 'Father' (10:21-22; 22:41-45; 23:34, 46). The intimacy with God that prayer provides is something Jesus wants to share with his disciples, particularly as he teaches them what we have come to know as The Lord's Prayer (11:1-4). Prayer continues to link key events with divine purpose: prayer is about revealing and conforming the will of characters to God's will. It is the privileged moment of encounter between human freedom and Divine will.

of cross-examining prosecutor. The desert is therefore a proving ground for the assertion that Jesus is 'Son of God' and, more importantly, a place for testing what that means. This is a good example of where we need to be cautious in imposing our pre-suppositions on Luke's story; the title 'Son of God' has for Christians today meaning developed over 2000 years of Christian theology that it did not have for the earliest Christians. Luke understands Jesus to be 'Son of God' in a unique way and his account of the temptations is one way in which be begins to unpack what it does and does not mean. In particular, does being 'Son of God' imply worldly advantages in terms of security, possessions and power?

That Jesus has been mysteriously sustained by the Holy Spirit during his time in the desert is implied by Luke's statement that he ate 'nothing at all during those days' (4:2). Humanly speaking, it is no wonder that he is famished. The devil's suggestion that he turn stones to bread seems to be a perfectly reasonable use of his power as 'Son of God' in such circumstances. But Jesus responds with a quotation: 'one does not live on bread alone' (Deut 8:3), indicating that to eat bread in the desert would show that bread is more fundamental for true life than the word of God. To be Son of God does not mean the use of divine power for one's own benefit, no matter how reasonable in human terms. To be Son of God means that one's true source and sustainer of life is God himself.

In the second temptation, the devil shows Jesus all the kingdoms of the world, offering to give them all to him in return for worship. Since Luke has already told us that Jesus, as Son of the Most High, may expect to be given the 'throne of his ancestor David' and rule over an everlasting kingdom (1:32-33), it may seem perfectly reasonable that Jesus should now grab the opportunity that the devil presents. Why fight with the devil if one can come to a compromise? The temptation is thus a cunning one: Jesus is a king – but what kind of shape will his kingdom have, and will it be given him by God or by the devil? Jesus' response 'worship the Lord your God, and serve only him' shows that to be 'Son of God' means a relationship of total fidelity to the Father. Divine sonship is not a means to worldly glory, but an end in itself.

The third and last temptation is particularly dreadful. Jesus has told the devil that as Son of God his relationship to the Father is one of total trust and fidelity. Not to be dissuaded by this, the devil opens a clever counter-attack: instead of appealing to basic human drives such as hunger and ambition, the devil himself quotes from the word of God! Quoting from Psalm 91, the devil argues that the one who, like Jesus, entrusts himself to God is entitled to expect protection from harm.

The temptation is subtle in the extreme: to do what the devil suggests will not be, like turning stones to bread, to deny the sufficiency of God's word for preserving life, but actually proving the point! To throw himself from a high building in reliance on the promise of protection would surely be to prove what Jesus himself has just affirmed. But Jesus replies with a quote from Deuteronomy 6:16, which makes it clear that the word of God is not to be trifled with in this way. As the Gospel will demonstrate, God's protection for his faithful servants is not to be understood in any naïve sense as simply protection from physical harm. To be Son of God is not to be exempt from human suffering.

At the end of the temptations scene, Luke adds an ominous note: the devil departs, but only until an 'opportune time' (4:13). This opportune time will not occur until the beginning of the Passion, when we will be told that 'Satan entered into Judas Iscariot' (22:3). Once again, Luke hints that the story that is to unfold will involve conflict and division.

Luke's account of the baptism, genealogy and temptations confirms and develops what the birth stories hinted at: that Jesus is in some unique way 'Son' of God. The relationship between Jesus and the Holy Spirit, first announced by the angel Gabriel, is shown continuing in the life of the adult Jesus. He is the beloved Son and the bearer of the Spirit. However, it becomes clear that Jesus is no mere passive tool of the Holy Spirit since his sonship and fidelity to the Father's will are put to the test.

Did you know:

- That only Luke tells us that Jesus was about thirty years old when he began his public ministry?
- That the baptism, genealogy and temptations of Jesus show what it means to be 'Son of God'?
- That some people thought that John the Baptist was the 'Messiah'?

Ministry in Galilee: Divided Opinion about Jesus (Luke 4:14-8:56)

16 When he came to Nazareth, where he had been brought up, he went to the synagogue on the sabbath day, as was his custom. He stood up to read, 17 and the scroll of the prophet Isaiah was given to him. He unrolled the scroll and found the place where it was written: 18 'The Spirit of the Lord is upon me, because he has anointed me to bring good news to the poor. He has sent me to proclaim release to the captives and recovery of sight to the blind, to let the oppressed go free, 19 to proclaim the year of the Lord's favour.'
20 And he rolled up the scroll, gave it back to the attendant, and sat down. The eyes of all in the synagogue were fixed on him. 21 Then he began to say to them, 'Today this scripture has been fulfilled in your hearing.'
(Luke 4:16-21)

Until this point in the story, the coming of the Son of God among his chosen people has remained largely hidden. As readers of Luke's story, we have been 'let in on' aspects of Jesus' identity of which only a few characters *within* the story are aware. As Jesus begins his public ministry of preaching and healing in Israel, we look on from a privileged vantage point, wondering whether what we know will become clear to others. Something of the drama to follow has already been hinted at by Simeon in the Temple. As he takes the infant Jesus in his arms he represents Israel's welcome of its Messiah, but he also prophesies that Jesus will be the cause of division in Israel ('the falling and the rising of many') and hints that the Gentiles may accept him (2:29-35). The next part of Luke's story (4:14-8:56) begins to bear out the truth of Simeon's predictions as Jesus begins his ministry in Galilee.

Luke's statement that Jesus began to teach in the synagogues of Galilee and was 'praised by everyone' suggests a positive beginning (4:15), but the very first incident narrated in any detail shows Jesus as the 'sign to be opposed': his own neighbours in Nazareth seek to take his life (4:16-30). By contrast, in the lakeside town of Capernaum, Jesus is welcomed with such enthusiasm that the townspeople want to prevent him leaving them (4:31-42)! The rise and fall of many in Israel has begun.

'NO-GO' ZONE IN NAZARETH

While Matthew, Mark and Luke all recount a visit to Nazareth that results in Jesus' rejection by his neighbours, Luke's version is quite distinctive. Matthew and Mark tell the story only after Jesus' ministry has already been in progress for some time, while Luke suggests that it is the first key event of that ministry. Luke alone tells us what Jesus said in the synagogue that so upset the townspeople, and it is only in Luke's version that they actually try to kill Jesus. The result is that in Luke's Gospel, violent opposition to Jesus arises right at the very beginning of his ministry.

Luke begins his story by reminding us that Nazareth is the place where Jesus had been brought up (4:16). We are invited to cast our minds back to the birth stories; this was the very place that the Lord's angel appeared to Mary. This insignificant village has already been a place of divine revelation. *We* know from the story so far that Jesus is 'great', 'Son of the Most High', the heir to the throne of

---

THE HEBREW WORD 'MESSIAH' (TRANSLATED INTO GREEK AS 'CHRIST') COMES FROM THE VERB 'TO ANOINT' AND THIS IS THE VERY WORD USED BY ISAIAH AND QUOTED BY JESUS HERE. THAT IS, JESUS CLAIMS TO HAVE BEEN 'MESSIAH-ED' OR 'CHRIST-ED' BY THE SPIRIT.

David, 'holy', 'Son of God' and 'Messiah'. But Jesus' own townspeople – the very people with whom he has been brought up and who should know him best – appear to know nothing of this, but think of Jesus simply as 'Joseph's son' (4:22). The rejection of Nazareth has implications for the whole story: if Jesus' own townspeople do not accept him as Messiah, what hope can there be for Israel in general?

The key to the scene in the synagogue is the passage from Isaiah 61:1-2 that Jesus reads (4:18-19). In the first place, it is the first public announcement of Jesus' Messiah-ship. The prophecy of Isaiah, Jesus says, has been fulfilled 'in the hearing' of those in the synagogue; in other words, Jesus is not just reading a prophecy about someone else, but applies it to *himself*. Thus, Jesus claims that the 'Spirit of the Lord' has 'anointed' him. The Hebrew word 'Messiah' (translated into Greek as 'Christ') comes from the verb 'to anoint' and this is the very word used by Isaiah and quoted by Jesus here. That is, Jesus claims to have been 'Messiah-ed' or 'Christ-ed' by the Spirit. The image of anointing by the Spirit is an unusual one. In the Old Testament, priests, prophets and kings could all be anointed with olive oil as a sign of their office, but those who were specially blessed could also experience being enveloped by God's Spirit, empowering them for their ministry.

The quote also says something about the kind of Messiah that Jesus will be. We have just mentioned that Old Testament 'messiahs' or 'anointed ones' could include priests, prophets and kings. By the time of Jesus, many Jews expected that God would send a new 'Messiah' who would surpass all those of the past. Many of Jesus' contemporaries expected this Messiah to be a royal figure, a king, who would be a great military leader and drive out the Romans from the Holy Land while re-establishing the ancient monarchy of David. One of the big problems for the early Christians was to explain why their Messiah Jesus had so spectacularly failed in this respect; rather than drive out the Romans, Jesus had been executed by them!

While the early Christians believed that Jesus was the royal descendant of David, they tended to transfer the royal and military aspects of Jesus' messiah-ship to the heavenly sphere (Jesus 'reigns' in heaven) and then to the idea of the Second Coming (Jesus will return to earth in glory as a great warrior and judge). In addition, the Gospels, and Luke in particular, show Jesus acting very much like the ancient prophets who spoke publicly on God's behalf and performed works of power over sickness and nature to demonstrate God's action on behalf of the poor. These anointed prophets in the Old Testament were often persecuted and even put to death. Jesus' earthly life, then, looks like the life of a prophetic Messiah, and the fact that Jesus' first 'public' words in the Gospel come from one of the great prophets is probably Luke's way of showing that Jesus will be a prophetic kind of Messiah.

The people of Nazareth are at first ready enough to accept this – they speak well of Jesus and are astounded at his gracious words. However, there seems to be a natural expectation that Jesus, whom they consider their own, will use his gifts of prophecy and healing for the advantage of his family and friends (4:23). They are in fact jealous of the fact that Jesus has done amazing things in Capernaum before looking after his own neighbours first. In response, he compares himself with two of Israel's greatest early prophets, Elijah and Elisha, whose ministry took them not only beyond their own neighbours, but also beyond Israel itself.

But what inspires the murderous rage of the villagers? It cannot be simply that Jesus speaks about the ministry of the prophets to Gentiles; Jesus is doing no more than reciting events well known to them from scripture. What infuriates them, it seems, is the realisation that the prophet Jesus will not perform at their beck and call, and if they cannot have him, no one will! Jesus' provocative statement that no prophet is ever accepted in his hometown helps to explain, in scriptural terms, why Israel rejects her Messiah. She has always behaved like this, as the lives of the prophets attest!

A TRIP TO CAPERNAUM

Escaping from Nazareth, we next hear of Jesus visiting Capernaum, a town by the lakeside. The visits to Nazareth and Capernaum form a contrasting pair. Capernaum has already been mentioned, unexpectedly perhaps, in the synagogue at Nazareth: 'Do here also in your hometown the things we have heard you did at Capernaum.' As in Nazareth, Jesus visit to Capernaum begins with teaching in the synagogue on the Sabbath (4:31). Unlike in Nazareth, we never hear what the content of the teaching is. Instead, a series of opportunities present themselves for the effective proclamation of the Lord's year of favour in works rather than words.

This occurs dramatically as Jesus' attempt to teach is frustrated by the abrupt shrieking of a man with the spirit of an unclean demon (4:33-36). There is a demonic parody of Jesus' self-proclamation in Nazareth as the demon attests Jesus' identity: 'I know who you are, the Holy One of God'. On that score the demon is better informed than the people of Nazareth! Similarly, when the Sabbath day ends, Luke tells us that Jesus cast demons out of many people, who in each case shouted, 'You are the Son of God!' (4:41) Like the devil himself, the unclean spirits seek to use their knowledge as a way of manipulating Jesus. It is significant that Jesus' first work of power in the Gospel is that of liberating a person from the power of the demonic, from all that controls and binds and dehumanises. For Luke, the casting out of demons is one of the primary signs of the presence of the kingdom of God (see also 11:20).

Leaving the synagogue, Jesus goes to Simon's house where he finds Simon's mother-in-law suffering from fever

A Gospel for the Poor

Only in Luke's Gospel does Jesus' public ministry begin with the proclamation of Isaiah 61:1-2: 'The Spirit of the Lord is upon me, because he has anointed me to bring good news to the poor' (4:18). While all of the gospels portray Jesus as concerned for the poor, the Gospel of Luke has a particular focus on those who are without the power and wealth that counts for importance in the world's eyes.

The version of the Beatitudes that we find in Matthew speaks of blessing for those who are 'poor in spirit' and who 'hunger and thirst for righteousness' (Matt 5:3,6). Luke's version states quite frankly that it is simply those who are 'poor' and 'hungry' who are blessed. In the ancient worldview, where material wealth was considered a sign of divine blessing, and poverty and sickness a sign of disfavour, it is indeed 'good news for the poor' that the kingdom of God is theirs. Luke alone recounts the parable of the beggar Lazarus and the unnamed rich man whose lack of compassion for the poor at his doorstep results in a dramatic reversal of fortune in the hereafter (16:19-31). It is not that the rich are necessarily excluded from the kingdom, but they are exhorted to use their wealth generously towards those who have less. Jesus concludes the strange parable of the dishonest steward (16:1-13) by teaching his hearers to use money to 'make friends' with those who will be able to 'welcome you into the eternal homes'. A similar idea is at work in another passage unique to Luke where Jesus teaches that hospitality offered to 'the poor, the crippled, the lame and the blind' will be repaid 'at the resurrection of the righteous' (14:12-14).

Matthew, Mark and Luke each write about the rich young man who is saddened at the idea that he must give away all he has to the poor in order to follow Jesus. While Matthew and Mark say that the man went away, Luke leaves the story unfinished (18:23-24); the challenge to live in solidarity with the poor and to depend on God's providence rather than on money is left open.

It is clear, though, that riches pose a serious obstacle to entering the kingdom. Luke alone reports the extraordinary teaching of Jesus that 'none of you can become my disciple if you do not give up all your possessions' (14:33). Another parable unique to Luke concerns the 'rich fool' who stores up earthly treasures but foolishly neglects his relationship with God (12:13-21). Real poverty in the ancient world was nothing to romanticise about, and Luke never does so; but he also has a keen sense that 'life does not consist in an abundance of possessions' (13:15).

(4:38-39). We are probably meant to see the woman's condition as more similar to demonic possession than to physical sickness. Luke uses strong language; she is, literally 'bound in a great fever' and Jesus is described as 'rebuking' it: the same word used to describe exorcisms. Simon's mother-in-law also needs to be 'liberated' from an oppressive force. After her restoration, she responds with service. Such service is to be a distinctive characteristic of disciples in Luke.

It is little wonder that the crowds of villagers who witness Jesus' healing and liberating power want to prevent Jesus from leaving them (4:42). At first sight this appears to be a positive response, certainly more positive than the attempted murder by the villagers in Nazareth. And yet, at a deeper level, they are not so unalike. The people of Capernaum have experienced the authoritative teaching and authoritative casting out of what binds human beings in possession and sickness, and yet they also fail to recognise Jesus as the Messiah. Like the people of Nazareth, the people of Capernaum are jealous of the benefits Jesus can bring them and they want to keep him to themselves. As in Nazareth, Jesus must escape: a daybreak departure into the wilderness. Once again, Jesus aligns himself with God's purpose that impels him to be on the move (4:43)

GONE FISHIN'

1Once while Jesus was standing beside the lake of Gennesaret, and the crowd was pressing in on him to hear the word of God, 2he saw two boats there at the shore of the lake; the fishermen had gone out of them and were washing their nets. 3He got into one of the boats, the one belonging to Simon, and asked him to put out a little way from the shore. Then he sat down and taught the crowds from the boat. 4When he had finished speaking, he said to Simon, 'Put out into the deep water and let down your nets for a catch.' 5Simon answered, 'Master, we have worked all night long but have caught nothing. Yet if you say so, I will let down the nets.' 6When they had done this, they caught so many fish that their nets were beginning to break. 7So they signalled to their partners in the other boat to come and help them. And they came and filled both boats, so that they began to sink. 8But when Simon Peter saw it, he fell down at Jesus' knees, saying, 'Go away from me, Lord, for I am a sinful man!' 9For he and all who were with him were amazed at the catch of fish that they had taken; 10 and so also were James and John, sons of Zebedee, who were partners with Simon. Then Jesus said to Simon, 'Do not be afraid; from now on you will be catching people.' 11When they had brought their boats to shore, they left everything and followed him. (Luke 5: 1-11)

After these two contrasting scenes at Nazareth and Capernaum, Luke devotes the next few episodes in his story to showing how Jesus' ministry begins to form both a core group of supporters (his disciples) and a core group of opponents (the Pharisees and scribes). In Matthew and Mark, Jesus is merely passing by the lake when, apparently out of the blue, he calls two pairs of brothers to become his first disciples. Luke tells a more complex story (5:1-11). Jesus is not passing by, but stationed by the lake, preaching to the crowds. His contact with the fishermen is prompted by a need for a stage as the crowd presses upon him; he enlists Simon the fisherman, albeit unwittingly, in his preaching of the word by commandeering his boat.

Jesus continues preaching and only when he finishes does he turn to address Simon directly, now not only commandeering the boat, but also telling the professional fisherman how to do his job! Simon naturally objects in terms that emphasise the pointlessness of putting the nets down again: they have worked all night and caught nothing. Yet Simon agrees in the end. From impossibility comes abundance, a catch almost beyond the capabilities of the fishermen to bring it in. They are amazed and Jesus wittily makes Simon's profession a metaphor for the work of catching people.

The metaphor is particularly apt given that the reader has been asked to imagine a crowd pressing on Jesus by the lake: there is an overabundant catch of people waiting here right before Simon's eyes. We will not see Simon Peter hauling in the catch, however, until the beginning of the Acts (2:41, yet another sign of the way in which the Gospel is really only the first part of a two volume story.

Simon is the first person in Jesus' public ministry who really begins to 'get it' about Jesus. After a night of fruitless work, Jesus provides Simon and his partners with such a catch of fish as they can hardly get to shore. If the people of Nazareth and Capernaum wanted to monopolise the benefits they perceive Jesus can bring, how much more ought this apply to the professional fisherman? Shekel signs ought to be floating before Simon's eyes. Yet Simon reacts in exactly the opposite way; he falls to the ground and says, 'Go away from me Lord, for I am a sinful man.' Simon is the first human being in the narrative to address Jesus as 'Lord' and at the same time he characterises himself as 'sinful'. Simon Peter is not perfect: indeed his imperfection will become all too evident.

This is vitally important to Luke's story, since it establishes the kind of people to whom Jesus specially directs his ministry. In fact, the narrative will turn almost immediately to the question of Jesus' authority to deal with sin (5:17-26 – healing of the paralytic) and his preference for associating with sinners, those who need to hear his call to repentance (5:27-32 – call of Levi). Jesus does not deny Simon's self-characterisation as sinful, but reassures him that it's no obstacle to being in Jesus' company as his disciple.

A universal message

Most people today probably think of 'Christ' as something like a surname for Jesus, but the word 'Christ' is in fact not a surname but a title meaning 'Anointed'. The Greek word Christos ('Christ') translates the Hebrew mashiach ('Messiah'). In other words, the earliest 'Christian' title for Jesus is a thoroughly Jewish one; Jesus was the long expected Messiah, the one anointed (and thus commissioned) by God to inaugurate God's kingdom.

Of course Jesus' disciples and the other earliest believers in Jesus as Messiah were Jews; they understood the coming of Jesus to be the fulfillment of the expectations of the people of Israel. Some parts of the New Testament, such as the Gospel of Matthew, seem to be written for communities of believers that were almost entirely Jewish. At the beginning it must have seemed to many that the 'good news' about Jesus was really good news only for Jews; after all, Jesus was the Jewish 'Messiah'. The beautiful canticles of the Magnificat (1:46-55) and the Benedictus (1:68-79) illustrate something of Jewish expectations about the coming of the Messiah.

However, two things became clear in the early decades after the death and resurrection of Jesus. First, that the vast majority of Jews were not able to be convinced that Jesus was truly the Messiah (largely because of his scandalous death as a criminal). Second, that there was unexpected interest in the good news about Jesus amongst non-Jews (Gentiles). Some early missionaries, such as Paul and his companions, discovered that the Gentiles were not only receptive to their message about Jesus but were also receiving the gift of the Holy Spirit in the same way as Jews who came to faith in Jesus as Messiah.

One of the questions that Luke tries to answer in his gospel is how the message about Jesus, the Jewish Messiah, could possibly be relevant to non-Jews. Many scholars think that the person to whom the Gospel and Acts are dedicated, Theophilus, was himself a Gentile. Luke wants to show that the good news about Jesus did not come to the Gentiles by accident or as a kind of back-up plan after the evangelisation of Jews had run into difficulty. Almost as a balance to the Magnificat and Benedictus in the birth stories, we hear Simeon – a model of Jewish faith and devo-

tion – proclaiming in the Nunc dimittis (2:29-32) that the infant Messiah will also be 'a light for revelation to the Gentiles' and the source of salvation 'prepared in the presence of all peoples'.

In other words, God planned for the Gentiles to be involved from the beginning! The theme of God's care for non-Jews runs through the Gospel. In his first public preaching at Nazareth, Jesus reminds his listeners that even in the Old Testament, God sent the prophets Elijah and Elisha to heal and care for Gentiles who demonstrated trust in the God of Israel (4:25-27). Jesus recalls the story of the salvation of the people of the Assyrian city of Nineveh as a result of their repentant response to the prophet Jonah (11:29-32). He teaches that the kingdom of God is open to people who 'will come from east and west, from north and south' and not only to those who belong to Israel (13:29-30). Jesus heals the servant of a Roman centurion and is so impressed with the Gentile soldier's trust that he exclaims, 'Not even in Israel have I found such faith' (7:9).

Luke is also particularly interested in the Samaritans, a people who were especially despised by many Jews at the time; even Jesus' own disciples want to call down fire from heaven upon a Samaritan village (9:54). Jesus not only rebukes his disciples, but he is also shown healing a Samaritan leper who, although a 'foreigner' in Jesus' eyes, returns to give thanks and praise to God for his cure (17:11-19). Only in Luke's Gospel do we find the parable of the 'Good Samaritan': a contradiction in terms for Jesus' Jewish contemporaries. The message is clear: if even Samaritans can be praised by Jesus for their faith and for their charity, then there seem to be no limits to those for whom the good news is intended.

At the end of the gospel, the risen Jesus tells his disciples that 'repentance and forgiveness of sins is to be proclaimed in his name to all nations beginning from Jerusalem' (24:47). Most of the Acts of the Apostles (from chapter ten onwards) is concerned with how the early believers carry out this instruction and take the good news even to the heart of the Roman Empire itself.

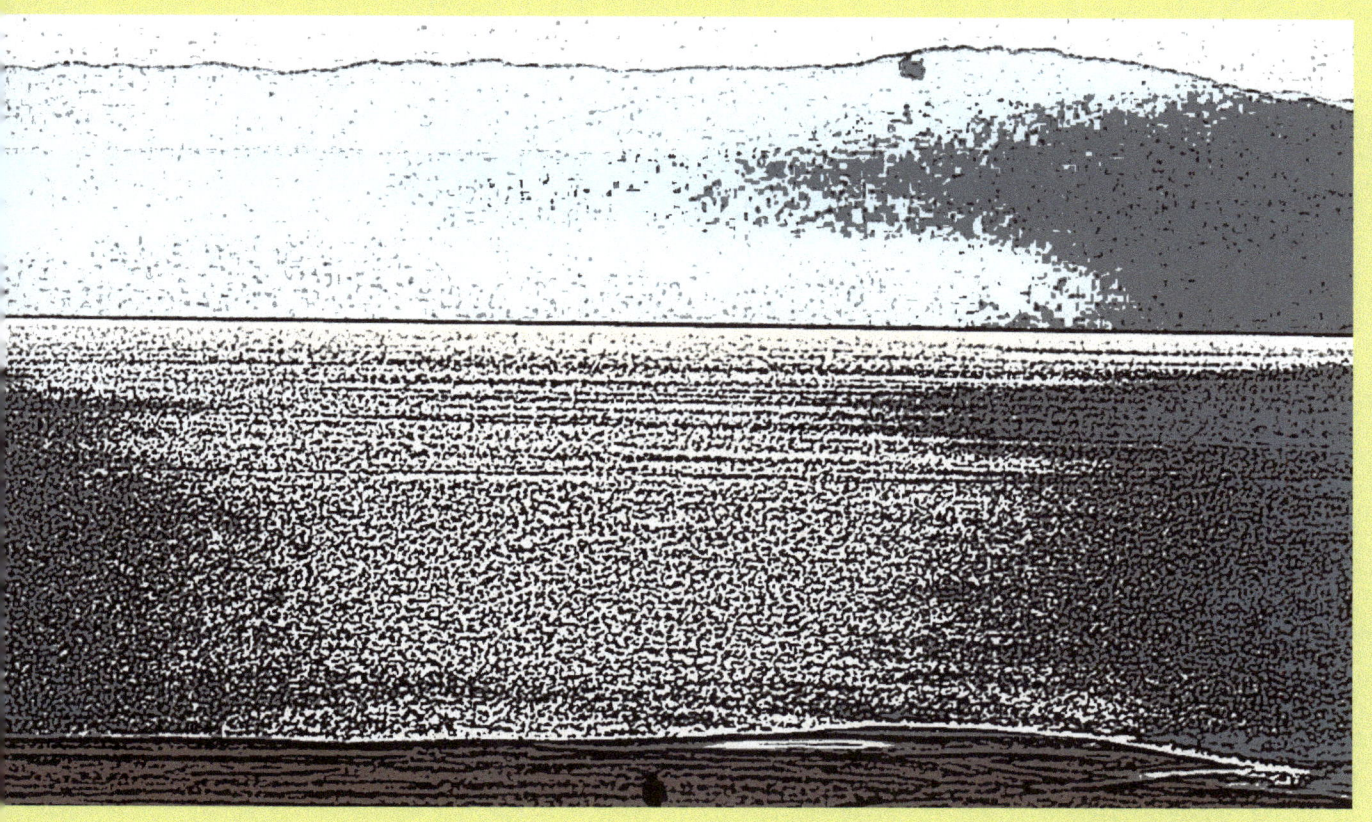

LEARNING ON THE JOURNEY

The word 'disciple' simply means a 'learner' and much of this section of the Gospel is concerned with Jesus gathering his disciples as they listen to his teaching (in particular, the so-called 'Sermon on the Plain': 6:17-49) and observe his prophetic actions as he heals, raises the dead and associates with sinners. Of these 'learners', Jesus will specially choose twelve to become 'apostles', that is, as those 'sent forth' to do the same as they have seen their master doing (6:12-16).

Almost immediately following the call of the first disciples, however, Luke introduces a group of opponents, the Pharisees and scribes, and so continues developing the theme of the rise and fall of many in Israel (5:17). The healing of a paralysed man presents an occasion for Jesus to assert that he not only casts out demons and heals physical illness, but that he can also forgive sin on God's behalf. In the context of Jesus' own culture, this is an extraordinary claim. 'Sin', by definition, is an offence against God and so the Pharisees are entirely right when they exclaim, 'Who can forgive sins but God alone?' (5:21) The Pharisees are shown debating with and testing both Jesus and his disciples from 5:17-6:11.

Despite this, we should recognise that Luke's Gospel does not demonise the Pharisees. They are presented as genuinely pious and motivated to do God's will; if they have a fault it is that they sometimes fail to root their piety in love for their brothers and sisters. In Luke, the Pharisees never plot to take Jesus' life and they play no part in the happenings in Jerusalem leading up to Jesus' death.

While the focus of Jesus' ministry in Galilee is his own people of Israel, there are glimpses of the opening of salvation to those beyond Israel, the Gentiles. The possibility that the Gentiles might be given the gift of faith is shown vividly in the account of the healing of a Roman centurion's servant (7:1-10). Jesus' declaration that the Roman's faith exceeds that of any found in Israel suggests an openness also on the Gentiles' part to Jesus' ministry. Jesus himself moves briefly across the lake into Gentile territory to exorcise the Gerasene demoniac (8:26-39); here, the Gentiles are afraid and yet Jesus commissions the restored man as a missionary to his own people. As yet, however, a mission to the Gentiles remains something for the future. Once again, we need to read the Acts of the Apostles to find out how this story ends.

Disciples Share in Jesus' Ministry (Luke 9:1-50)

WHAT TO DO IN GALILEE

Chapters four to nine of Luke's Gospel tell the story of Jesus' ministry of authoritative words and works in Galilee. The plot is marked by a developing division within Israel in response to Jesus. Jesus, whom the reader knows to be the Messiah, is characterised in prophetic terms and thus Israel's traditional opposition to her prophets will also mark the ministry of Jesus, beginning with his own townspeople in Nazareth. Opposition also emerges from demonic forces and from the scribes and Pharisees. On the other hand, the 'crowds' are favourable, sometimes even too enthusiastic. Disciples are called and told that they will be 'catching people', although they recede largely into the background in chapters five to eight – in this section they are students of Jesus, listening to what Jesus teaches and observing his works.

Luke's final chapter in Galilee, chapter nine, is a pivotal one for the story of the Gospel. Here, Luke shows the disciples beginning to play the role promised by Jesus to Peter: that they would become fishers for people. In coming to see that Jesus is the Messiah, the disciples have come to an understanding beyond that of the crowds. But they do not yet understand that the prophetic Messiah must suffer a prophet's death, a death that will be associated with Jerusalem.

The inner group of the disciples, 'the twelve', are commissioned by Jesus to imitate his own ministry by proclaiming the kingdom of God and healing (9:1-6). Their successful ministry, however, draws the attention of the authorities of another kingdom, that of Herod. He wants to know who is behind the strange goings-on in his territory and is particularly disturbed by the rumours that John the Baptist, whom he beheaded, has risen from the dead (9:7-9).

At this point, we are supposed to be shocked; nothing in Luke's story so far has hinted at John's grisly end. In chapter seven, John was still alive and well, though presumably still in prison (3:19-20), since he sends messengers to Jesus. Now we are suddenly told that he has been executed, though Luke never tells us how this happens (contrast Matt 14:3-12 and Mark 6:17-29). Herod, it seems, is a dangerously unstable character and his growing interest in the identity of Jesus can therefore be no good thing. Eventually he will play a part in the trial of Jesus in Jerusalem, an involvement only Luke mentions (23:6-12). For the first time in the Gospel since the attempt of the villagers in Nazareth to throw him over the cliff, there is an indication that Jesus could be in mortal danger.

18 Once when Jesus* was praying alone, with only the disciples near him, he asked them, 'Who do the crowds say that I am?' 19They answered, 'John the Baptist; but others, Elijah; and still others, that one of the ancient prophets has arisen.' 20He said to them, 'But who do you say that I am?' Peter answered, 'The Messiah of God.'
21 He sternly ordered and commanded them not to tell

> IN COMING TO SEE THAT JESUS IS THE MESSIAH, THE DISCIPLES HAVE COME TO AN UNDERSTANDING BEYOND THAT OF THE CROWDS. BUT THEY DO NOT YET UNDERSTAND THAT THE PROPHETIC MESSIAH MUST SUFFER A PROPHET'S DEATH, A DEATH THAT WILL BE ASSOCIATED WITH JERUSALEM.

GOD'S WILL AND HUMAN FREEDOM

The story of the finding of the child Jesus in the Temple ends with Jesus asking the enigmatic question, 'Did you not know that I must be in my Father's house?' (2:49). As he begins his public ministry, Jesus tells his first disciples, 'I must proclaim the good news of the kingdom of God to the other cities also; for I was sent for this purpose' (4:43). And, as he prepares to make his way to Jerusalem, Jesus also tells them, 'The Son of Man must undergo great suffering, and be rejected by the elders, chief priests, and scribes, and be killed, and on the third day be raised' (9:22).

These are the first uses in the Gospel of the little Greek word *dei* which means 'must' or 'it is/was necessary'. It's a word that Luke uses a lot in his Gospel and even more in the Acts of the Apostles. Very often, as in these three examples, Luke wants to convey the idea that something had to happen because God wanted it to happen. Luke has a particularly strong sense of what we might call the 'divine necessity' – the unstoppable unfolding of the divine plan, especially through the ministry of Jesus (in the Gospel) and then through the Church (in Acts).

An important question to consider as we read the story is: how does the divine purpose fit with human freedom? That human beings can turn away from the divine purpose is clear. The divine necessity is strangely unstoppable, but it does not overwhelm any individual who chooses to reject it. No one is forced to accept Jesus as the Messiah: his rejection and execution is proof enough of that. But even Jesus himself and his disciples show that their adherence to the divine purpose is ultimately free, since it is possible to turn away from it. While Jesus adheres to it after the testing in the desert and the agony in Gethsemane, Peter turns away for a time, and Judas does so permanently.

What the Gospel will show over and over again is that human beings can freely align themselves with the divine will through prayer. It is why Jesus himself prays on the Mount of Olives before his death and why he encourages his disciples also to pray which they fail to do and the consequences follow. Instead of free adherence to God's will, they fall victim to the forces of fear.

Mysteriously, though, the divine purpose itself seems to take account of the fact that it will encounter opposition and human failure. The very death of the Messiah, the ultimate opposition to God's visitation of his people, is not something that God has to fix up as an afterthought. Instead, it is presented as something that the divine plan encompassed, as the risen Jesus makes clear to the disciples on the road to Emmaus, 'was it not necessary that the Messiah should suffer these things and so enter into his glory?' (24:44) Luke's story is one of confidence in the fact that God's design for the salvation of all people cannot ultimately be frustrated.

28 Friendly Guide to Luke's Gospel

anyone, 22saying, 'The Son of Man must undergo great suffering, and be rejected by the elders, chief priests, and scribes, and be killed, and on the third day be raised.' 23 Then he said to them all, 'If any want to become my followers, let them deny themselves and take up their cross daily and follow me. 24For those who want to save their life will lose it, and those who lose their life for my sake will save it. 25What does it profit them if they gain the whole world, but lose or forfeit themselves? 26Those who are ashamed of me and of my words, of them the Son of Man will be ashamed when he comes in his glory and the glory of the Father and of the holy angels. 27But truly I tell you, there are some standing here who will not taste death before they see the kingdom of God.' 28 Now about eight days after these sayings Jesus took with him Peter and John and James, and went up on the mountain to pray. 29And while he was praying, the appearance of his face changed, and his clothes became dazzling white. 30Suddenly they saw two men, Moses and Elijah, talking to him. 31They appeared in glory and were speaking of his departure, which he was about to accomplish at Jerusalem. 32Now Peter and his companions were weighed down with sleep; but since they had stayed awake, they saw his glory and the two men who stood with him. 33Just as they were leaving him, Peter said to Jesus, 'Master, it is good for us to be here; let us make three dwellings, one for you, one for Moses, and one for Elijah'—not knowing what he said. 34While he was saying this, a cloud came and overshadowed them; and they were terrified as they entered the cloud. 35Then from the cloud came a voice that said, 'This is my Son, my Chosen; listen to him!' 36When the voice had spoken, Jesus was found alone. And they kept silent and in those days told no one any of the things they had seen. (Luke 9:18-36)

Herod's question about Jesus ('who is this about whom I hear such things?') is taken up in the important episodes of Peter's declaration about Jesus and the Transfiguration. The return of the twelve and the feeding of the five thousand (9:10-17) prompts Jesus to ask his disciples what the crowds are saying about him. They, like Herod, think of Jesus as a prophetic figure come back to life: John the Baptist, Elijah or another ancient prophet (9:19). They have had some insight in correctly identifying the prophetic nature of Jesus' ministry, but it remains for Peter to draw the correct conclusion from this: that Jesus is in fact the Messiah of God (9:20). Even Peter's assessment, though, needs to be correctly understood.

As we have already seen, the Messiah was widely expected to be a royal and military figure who would re-establish the kingdom of Israel. But Jesus is not a Messiah of this kind; he is the Messiah who proclaims and inaugurates the kingdom of God, which is not to be confused with any earthly kingdom. It is probably because of the likelihood of misunderstanding that Jesus forbids his disciples from telling anyone that he is the Messiah (9:21). The disciples themselves must come to see that the Messiah 'must undergo great suffering' (9:22) and even be prepared to share in it.

MOUNTAIN CLIMBING

The question of Jesus' identity is also the focus of the episode usually called the Transfiguration (9:28-36). The scene on the mountain is the climax of this part of the Gospel: Herod is bewildered as to Jesus' identity; Peter is correct, though with limited understanding; now God himself gives the fullest answer possible. Mountains were places of contact with the divine. The potential for this unidentified mountain to be a place of revelation is confirmed by the fact that Jesus intended to pray there. While praying, the appearance of Jesus' face is altered; Luke is probably alluding here to Moses' face shining after speaking with God on Mt Sinai (Exod 34:29).

There are numerous connections with Moses and the exodus from Egypt, the great saving event of the Old Testament. Not only does Moses himself appear, but they speak of Jesus' 'departure' (the Greek word is *exodos*). The cloud, too, alludes to the pillar of cloud that guided the Israelites on their march through the desert. Peter's delirious suggestion that he should build tents reminds us of the great tent, or tabernacle, which housed the ark of the covenant in the desert. All this suggests that just as God acted powerfully in the exodus to free his people, so now he acts again through Jesus to liberate and save.

The discussion with Moses and Elijah contributes to Luke's picture of Jesus as a prophetic Messiah; a Messiah whose message, like that of Moses and the prophets, will meet with opposition from within Israel itself. However, the episode on the mountain takes the question of Jesus' identity even further; Jesus is indeed a prophet, but this is only part of the truth about his identity. He is a prophet because he is first the 'Son' and thus the spokesman par excellence for God, as the divine voice itself affirms: 'This is my Son, the Chosen. Listen to him.' (9:35) While we readers have known since the beginning of the Gospel that Jesus is the 'Son of God', this is the first time that disciples have been let in on this vital piece of information.

The disciples' training for ministry has begun in earnest in chapter 9 and the reason for it is now becoming clear: Jesus is soon to *depart* from them, leaving them to carry on his ministry of proclamation of the kingdom. Unfortunately, the Twelve keep taking one step forward, two steps back. Given a share in Jesus' own authority (9:1-2), they enjoy success in proclamation and healing. Placing their faith in providence and taking nothing for the journey, they lack nothing. Immediately after their return, however, they seem to have taken none of this to heart since they suggest that the crowd be sent away to buy bread, and even when Jesus invites them to deepen their faith in providence they can only see their own inadequacy. A time of prayer in Jesus' company, however, allows Peter to move beyond the understanding of the crowds: Jesus is no ordinary prophet, but the Messiah. That Jesus forbids them to speak of this, however, indicates that they do not yet understand the implications of his Messiahship and so he explains the path of suffering he must travel.

> WHILE THE DISCIPLES TRY TO MAINTAIN THEIR 'EXCLUSIVE RIGHTS' OVER MINISTRY IN JESUS' NAME, JESUS RELATIVISES THEIR MINISTRY BY APPROVING OF ANYONE WHO USES HIS NAME TO CAST OUT DEMONS. THE DISCIPLES STILL HAVE MUCH TO LEARN ON THE WAY TO JERUSALEM.

Following the episode on the mountain, Jesus again tries to teach the disciples about his fate (9:44). Lack of perception, augmented by fear, prevents them from learning their lesson. They bicker among themselves as to who is the greatest; their argument has the distasteful look of 'succession planning' for when Jesus is gone. Jesus pointedly reminds them that their only 'greatness' comes from the fact that he commissions them; in fact, he could just as easily commission a child to do their work (9:46-48)! While the disciples try to maintain their 'exclusive rights' over ministry in Jesus' name, Jesus relativises their ministry by approving of anyone who uses his name to cast out demons. The disciples still have much to learn on the way to Jerusalem.

Telling Stories on the Way to Jerusalem (Luke 9:51-19:44)

In Luke 9:51 the story takes a dramatic turn. In the transfiguration scene we saw Moses and Elijah speaking to Jesus about his 'departure' which he was to accomplish in Jerusalem. Now we are told that 'when the days drew near for him to be taken up, he set his face for Jerusalem.' It is important for Luke that Jesus is not the mere victim of circumstances or the plotting of others; Jesus himself resolves to go to Jerusalem where he will not only face death, but also his mysterious 'departure' and 'ascension'. Numerous times throughout the next ten chapters, Luke will remind us that Jesus is 'on the way' as if to emphasise the deliberate nature of Jesus' journey (9:51, 53, 56, 57; 10:1, 38; 13:22, 33; 14:25; 17:11; 18:31, 35-36; 19:1, 11, 28, 29, 37, 41, 45).

In Luke's second volume, the Acts of the Apostles, we discover that the earliest Christians were called followers of 'the Way' (e.g. Acts 9:2). In drawing out Jesus' final journey from Galilee to Jerusalem over ten chapters, Luke is quite different from Mark and Matthew. In Matthew, Jesus leaves Galilee for Judea in chapter 19 and enters the Temple in chapter 21. Mark's account of the journey is even shorter (10:32-11:11).

These references to the 'way' lead many commentators on Luke's Gospel to think of this section of the Gospel as the 'journey to Jerusalem' or as Luke's 'travel narrative'. From this perspective, these ten chapters of the Gospel tell the story of this journey, culminating with Jesus' arrival in Jerusalem and re-entry to the Temple (19:45): the first time in the Gospel that Jesus appears in the Temple since his childhood. That said, the 'journey to Jerusalem' may not look like much of a story. There is no single overarching plot, except perhaps Jesus' goal of reaching Jerusalem. The interest in most stories lies in seeing how the hero overcomes obstacles as he or she attempts to achieve a goal.

In Jesus' journey to Jerusalem, very little actually happens compared with the drama-filled Galilean ministry (4:14-9:50). At least eleven individual healing and exorcism stories occur in the Galilean ministry, and in addition there are such works of power as the calming of the storm and feeding of the five thousand. In the much longer travel narrative, there are no works of power over nature and only five healing stories: an exorcism (11:14), the crippled woman (13:10-17), the man with dropsy (14:1-6), the ten lepers (17:11-19), and the blind beggar (18:35-43). At this point in the Gospel there is a sense that further miracles are a distraction; the crowds are attracted by them, but they show little understanding that the miracles point to a greater reality which is the kingdom of God coming upon them (11:20).

We know from Jesus himself that these are signs: he told the messengers from John the Baptist as much in 7:22. The crowds demand further signs (11:29-32), but fail to interpret the signs already given them (12:54-59). Instead of dramatic events such as healings and other miracles, the bulk of the story of the journey to Jerusalem

---

Most parables contain some element that is strange or unusual. They should cause us to say,
'Wait a minute: that's not how farmers do their work!
That's not what kings usually do!
That's not what normally happens in nature!'
And this strange element should
tease us into thought.

Parables in the travel narrative

Some parables from Jesus' journey to Jerusalem found only in Luke's Gospel:

Good Samaritan	Lk 10:25-37
Friend asking for help at midnight	Lk 11:5-8
Rich fool	Lk 12:16-21
Watchful slaves	Lk 12:35-38
Barren fig-tree	Lk 13:6-9
Narrow door	Lk 13:24-30
Taking the lowest place	Lk 14:7-11
Tower-builder & King planning for war	Lk 14:28-32
Lost coin	Lk 15:8-10
Prodigal son	Lk 15:11-32
Dishonest steward	Lk 16:1-8
Rich man & Lazarus	Lk 16:19-31
Widow and unjust judge	Lk 18:1-8
Pharisee & tax collector	Lk 18:9-14

is concerned with Jesus teaching his disciples and preparing them for what will happen. Those who wish to follow Jesus on the way to Jerusalem are warned not to take the decision lightly (9:57-61; 14:25-33). Disciples are cautioned about the fate of unfaithful servants and reminded that Jesus has come not to bring peace but 'fire to the earth' (12:41-53).

A GUIDED TOUR

Strikingly, a massive part of Jesus' teaching in these chapters is in the form of parables, many of which are themselves stories in miniature. Thus, in Luke's travel narrative, Jesus moves from being a miracle-worker to a storyteller. Some years ago C.H. Dodd coined what has become a classic definition of 'parable':

At its simplest a parable is a metaphor or simile drawn from nature or common life, arresting the hearer by its vividness or strangeness, and leaving the mind in sufficient doubt about its precise application to tease it into active thought.

Although all the Gospels contain parables of Jesus, Luke's Gospel is especially rich in them. Luke adds to the parables he takes over from Mark and those he shares

with Matthew; indeed many of Luke's parables are found nowhere else. Among these are some of the most famous: the Good Samaritan, the Places of Honour at the Wedding Banquet, the Prodigal Son, the Rich Man and Lazarus, the Pharisee and the Publican. These are concentrated above all in Luke's account of the journey to Jerusalem.

The meaning of most parables is not obvious. If we assume we know what Jesus is talking about, we are probably missing the main point; if we are too familiar with the story, we might not think carefully enough about its real meaning. Most parables contain some element that is strange or unusual. They should cause us to say, 'Wait a minute: that's not how farmers do their work! That's not what kings usually do! That's not what normally happens in nature!' And this strange element should tease us into thought.

While each parable needs to be seen within its own particular context, there is a certain thematic link running through many of the principal parables in the journey to Jerusalem. God is presented as abundantly, even ridiculously, gracious. Many of these parables seem to be directed at breaking down an image of an ungenerous God, a God who can and must be manipulated. The parables suggest that God is not a tyrant or a pitiless judge, but rather a Father who is completely in love with his children. Perhaps the best known of all Jesus' parables is the one commonly known as the parable of the 'Prodigal Son' (15:11-32). This is one of the parables found only in Luke's Gospel and it occurs almost mid-way through the journey to Jerusalem. Since it is impossible here to go through all of the parables Jesus tells while on the way to Jerusalem, let's look a little more closely at the parable of the Prodigal Son, particularly as it is representative of the key theme of the generous and gracious God.

1 Now the tax collectors and sinners were all gathering around to hear Jesus. 2 But the Pharisees and the teachers of the law muttered, "This man welcomes sinners and eats with them."

3 Then Jesus told them this parable: 4 "Suppose one of you has a hundred sheep and loses one of them. Doesn't he leave the ninety-nine in the open country and go after the lost sheep until he finds it? 5 And when he finds it, he joyfully puts it on his shoulders 6 and goes home. Then he calls his friends and neighbors together and says, 'Rejoice with me; I have found my lost sheep.' 7 I tell you that in the same way there will be more rejoicing in heaven over one sinner who repents than over ninety-nine righteous persons who do not need to repent.
The Parable of the Lost Coin

8 "Or suppose a woman has ten silver coins[a] and loses one. Doesn't she light a lamp, sweep the house and search carefully until she finds it? 9 And when she finds it, she calls her friends and neighbors together and says, 'Rejoice with me; I have found my lost coin.' 10 In the same way, I tell you, there is rejoicing in the presence of the angels of God over one sinner who repents."

11 Jesus continued: "There was a man who had two sons. 12 The younger one said to his father, 'Father, give me my share of the estate.' So he divided his property between them.

13 "Not long after that, the younger son got together all he had, set off for a distant country and there squandered his wealth in wild living. 14 After he had spent everything, there was a severe famine in that whole country, and he began to be in need. 15 So he went and hired himself out to a citizen of that country, who sent him to his fields to feed pigs. 16 He longed to fill his stomach with the pods that the pigs were eating, but no one gave him anything.

17 "When he came to his senses, he said, 'How many of my father's hired servants have food to spare, and here I am starving to death! 18 I will set out and go back to my father and say to him: Father, I have sinned against heaven and against you. 19 I am no longer worthy to be called your son; make me like one of your hired servants.' 20 So he got up and went to his father.

"But while he was still a long way off, his father saw him and was filled with compassion for him; he ran to his son, threw his arms around him and kissed him.

21 "The son said to him, 'Father, I have sinned against heaven and against you. I am no longer worthy to be called your son.'

22 "But the father said to his servants, 'Quick! Bring the best robe and put it on him. Put a ring on his finger and sandals on his feet. 23 Bring the fattened calf and kill it. Let's have a feast and celebrate. 24 For this son of mine was dead and is alive again; he was lost and is found.' So they began to celebrate.

25 "Meanwhile, the older son was in the field. When he came near the house, he heard music and dancing. 26 So he called one of the servants and asked him what was going on. 27 'Your brother has come,' he replied, 'and your father has killed the fattened calf because he has him back safe and sound.'

28 "The older brother became angry and refused to go in. So his father went out and pleaded with him. 29 But he answered his father, 'Look! All these years I've been slaving for you and never disobeyed your orders. Yet you never gave me even a young goat so I could celebrate with my friends. 30 But when this son of yours who has squandered your property with prostitutes comes home, you kill the fattened calf for him!'

> THE THREE PARABLES OF THE LOST THINGS THEMSELVES CULMINATE IN PARTIES TO CELEBRATE THE RECOVERY OF WHAT WAS LOST; IN THE CASE OF THE LOST SON, THERE IS A SPLENDID BARBECUE WITH THE 'FATTED CALF'!

31 "'My son,' the father said, 'you are always with me, and everything I have is yours. 32 But we had to celebrate and be glad, because this brother of yours was dead and is alive again; he was lost and is found.'"

The first thing we should notice about the parable is that it comes straight after two short parables about lost things: a sheep (15:3-7) and a coin (15:8-10). This suggests that we should think of the next parable not as the parable of the Prodigal Son, but the parable of the Lost Son. All these parables are about recovering what has been lost. But why tell these parables at all? What is their point? By giving us the context for the three parables, 15:1-2 helps us to answer those questions. The parables are directed at the 'Pharisees and scribes' who grumble that Jesus welcomes and eats with public sinners and tax collectors.

In ancient Mediterranean culture, eating was a sign of communion. To eat with sinners was in some sense to identify with them, to be on their level, and the Pharisees and scribes find this scandalous. This part of the Gospel is full of references to meals: in 14:1-24 Jesus eats in the home of a leading Pharisee where he tells parables about taking the lowest place and about a great dinner. The three parables of the lost things themselves culminate in parties to celebrate the recovery of what was lost; in the case of the lost son, there is a splendid barbecue with the 'fatted calf'!

Soon after the parables of the lost things, Jesus tells another parable about a rich man who feasted sumptuously everyday but had not so much as a scrap for the poor man, Lazarus, at his door (16:19-31). Given the number of meals that Jesus has had with the Pharisees (7:36-50; 11:53; 14:1-24), their grumbling has an air of pettiness. Nor have they taken to heart the teaching of Jesus that the ideal dinner guests are those on the margins of society. Jesus apparently tells these parables to justify his behaviour in eating with those whom the establishment marginalises.

Of the three parables of the lost things, the parable of the Lost Son speaks most directly to the situation. The father welcomes back his son, a sinner, and eats with him, while the older brother grumbles about it. The two shorter parables serve as guides to the interpretation of the longer one, since it is only in the shorter parables that Jesus gives a theological explanation of the stories: like the man and woman who lost possessions and then recovered them, so God and the heavenly company rejoice when a sinner repents. God ('heaven') is symbolised by the one who loses something; the sinner is symbolised by what is lost.

The parable of the lost son is not exactly the same as those of the lost sheep and lost coin, however. In the first place, we might notice that the stakes are progressively increased: the sheep is only one in a hundred, the coin

TELLING STORIES ON THE WAY TO JERUSALEM 35

is one in ten, but the lost son is only one of two. The biggest difference between the parables, though, is in what happens after the lost son is recovered. It is only in this parable that someone refuses to join in with the general rejoicing. While the first section of the parable (15:11-24) parallels the parables of the sheep and coin by focusing on what has been lost and found, the second section (15:25-32) is totally new. Here, the focus is on the older brother who refuses to acknowledge that finding something that was lost is reason for celebration. It is of course at this very point that the parable addresses the situation of the grumbling Pharisees and scribes.

IN THE DETAILS

It's time now to have a closer look at the parable itself. In 15:11 three characters are introduced: a father and his two sons. Family relationships are central to this parable; as you read it, try to pay attention to the way terms such as 'father', 'son', and 'brother' are used. Notice the contrast between these words that imply freedom and love, and words implying a relationship of servitude or slavery. Since the parable implicitly compares the Pharisees and scribes to the elder son and the sinners and tax collectors to the younger son, Jesus also implies that all these people are in fact 'brothers'. Part of the problem for the Pharisees and scribes is that they no longer recognise those whom they characterise as 'sinners' as their brothers and sisters.

Jesus creates a thoroughly unattractive picture of the younger son – this young man is not a loveable character. We are not meant to feel sorry for him, but to be repulsed by him. In 15:12 he makes an extraordinary and presumptuous request of his father: to divide up the family property prior to his father's death. His request deals a mortal blow to his relationship with his father; he effectively tells his father that the father is as good as dead. The father himself will later acknowledge that the action cuts both ways: as a result of his request, the younger son became 'dead' to his father too (15:24, 32). Despite the insult, the father is remarkably passive. Instead of exercising his authority over his son, the father simply gives in.

The way Jesus describes the father is consistently at odds with expectations of how the patriarch of an ancient Middle Eastern family should act. He will be moved with compassion for his lost son, he will put aside his dignity and go running from the house to meet him as he returns, he will also leave the house and plead with his other son.

The description of what the younger son does next would also have resounded even more negatively with a Jewish audience. He travels to a distant country, abandoning the holy land of Israel to live among the Gentiles. While there he recklessly squanders his property; almost unbelievably, he spends *everything*. His own recklessness then combines with the circumstances of famine to force him into servitude and, most disgustingly of all, to live among pigs. By this stage the younger son is totally cut off from his own people and starving – as good as dead in every sense.

At this point he 'came to himself' (15:17): for the first time we get a hint that the greed and folly of this young man are not the sum total of his personality. In the depths of his being, he remains a 'son' in relationship with a 'father'. Realising that he has done wrong and that his situation compares unfavourably with that of his father's servants, he resolves to return. However, despite his repentance, he has given up hope of being accepted back as a son and will accept the status of a hired hand. Compare this with the older son who sees himself as no better than a slave. At this low ebb of the story, there is a dramatic turning point. Luke's original Greek literally says, '*rising*, he went to his father': this son will rise from the dead (15:20).

Unlike the case of the shepherd and the woman in the preceding parables, there is no description of the father's search for his son. However, the father sees the son while a long way off, suggesting that the father is on the lookout. At the mere sight of his son on the horizon, the father swings into action. All dignity is forgotten as he leaves his proper place, which is to wait for the son to come to him and beg forgiveness. He doesn't walk, but runs, and the father 'falls upon him' with hugs and kisses. In imagining this tender scene, we should keep in mind that the son is not only in a physically filthy condition but, given that he has been in Gentile territory and amongst pigs, he is certainly ritually unclean – all good reasons for his father to exercise some restraint in his contact. The son then attempts to give his prepared speech, but is unable to finish – he never gets as far as asking to be relegated to the status of a servant – because his father interrupts with a series of orders to those who are truly servants. The robe, sandals and ring together symbolise the restoration of the son to his place in the family. The link to the previous parables of 'lost and found' is made by the father who describes his son in these very terms (15:24).

As with the preceding parables, the recovery of the lost is followed by a celebration. Once again, there is an escalation in this parable: at the heart of the celebration is the consumption of the fattened calf. This is a calf specially (and expensively) fed on grain, probably for market. Such an animal has been estimated to be able to provide enough meat for up to seventy-five people: this will be a big barbecue! We are reminded that the context for the parables is an accusation that Jesus eats with sinners. In the father's terms, such a feast is the appropriate response to the recovery of a son who was as good as dead (15:23-24).

At this point the older son comes on the scene (15:25). Many readers today, and probably the original audience, feel some sympathy with the older brother. Within his culture, he, unlike the father, reacts in the expected way: his younger brother has deliberately disgraced the family and deserves to be shunned. When the older son angrily refuses to come in for the celebration, the father is again portrayed in a way contrary to expectations. The father would be entitled simply to send a servant with a demand that his son come inside. Instead, he leaves the celebration and reduces himself to 'pleading' (15:28). The scene is bitterly ironic as the older son protests that he has never disobeyed his father's command, and yet his 'refusal to go in' flies in the face of his father's 'pleading'. It appears that the older son is quite capable of disobedience, of becoming a 'sinner' in lack of respect for his father.

> IT APPEARS THAT A NECESSARY PART OF THE COMING OF THE KINGDOM OF GOD IS THE CELEBRATION OF THE RETURN OF REPENTANT SINNERS AND HENCE OF EATING AND DRINKING WITH THEM.

Once again, there is an implied critique of the Pharisees and scribes here; is it not possible that they too are 'sinners'? We also discover something sad about the older son's relationship with his father: he sees himself not as a beloved son but as a slave (15:29). The younger son, for all his infamous behaviour, consistently addresses his father as 'Father', but the older son never does so! The father will contradict the older son, pointing out that he is anything but a slave: he shares in the ownership of everything that is the father's. At the same time, the older son dissociates himself from any relationship with his brother, calling him simply 'your son' and inventing a lurid account of the younger son's activities with prostitutes; the story gives no hint of this, and, in any case, how could the older brother know?

SINNING AND FORGIVENESS

For the third time in the parable, the father affirms the appropriateness of celebration for the lost son's return. Now, however, the father raises the celebration to the level of 'necessity': 'we *had* to celebrate and rejoice' (15:32). The parable ends abruptly on this note. It is not clear whether or not the older son joins in the celebration at the father's invitation, just as it remains unclear whether the Pharisees and scribes will join in the celebratory meals Jesus enjoys with their 'brothers': the tax collectors and sinners.

While this parable certainly highlights the father's (and thus, God's) forgiveness, it does more than that. The parable is not just about God's treatment of 'sinners', but about *our* treatment of those we so easily label 'sinners' or marginalise in other ways. The Pharisees and scribes, and we ourselves, are challenged to reflect on the different possible responses to the recovery of the lost: do we respond with compassion and celebration (as in the Father's case) or with resentment and 'anger' (as in the elder brother's case)? It appears that a necessary part of the coming of the kingdom of God is the celebration of the return of repentant sinners and hence of eating and drinking with them.

The parable of the Lost Son is only one example of the many parables that characterise Jesus' journey to Jerusalem. Hopefully, our reading of the parable has opened up one or more unexpected aspects of this well-known story. Some of the other parables found only in Luke are listed in the box. As you read them, try to put aside your assumptions and be open to the surprising elements of what Jesus has to say.

DID YOU KNOW?

- That the first Christians called themselves followers of 'the Way' (Acts 9:2)
- That the parables of the Prodigal Son, the Good Samaritan, and the Rich Man and Lazarus are only in Luke's Gospel?

Final days in Jerusalem
(Luke 19:45-23:56)

CAPITAL CITY

The story of the Passion itself – the betrayal and crucifixion of Jesus – really begins at Luke 22:1, but it is being prepared for from the moment Jesus enters Jerusalem. Jesus' popularity with the people as a whole, together with pointed criticism of their leaders, quickly results in a desire to kill him (19:47). Luke implies that Jesus spends several days in Jerusalem, constantly teaching in the precincts of the Temple (19:47; 21:37): a reminder that, once again, Jesus is 'in his Father's house' or 'in his Father's affairs'.

In chapter twenty, Jesus claims authority over the Temple and attracts the people to his side. At the same time, his activity threatens the Jerusalem leaders whom Jesus characterises as unfaithful tenants in a parable (20:9-19). They try and fail to defeat him in debates about the legitimacy of paying taxes to Rome and about the reality of the bodily resurrection (20:20-40). Increasingly, they turn to plots of violence but are unable to penetrate the protective barrier around Jesus formed by the people (19:48; 20:19, 26). In chapter twenty-one, Jesus' preaching takes a dramatic turn as he speaks of the destruction of the Temple itself and the mysterious coming of the 'Son of Man' (21:5-28).

The Passion account in Luke is one of the most detailed sections of the Gospel: a full two chapters are devoted to the last twenty-four hours or so of Jesus' earthly life. Unlike much of the Gospel, which consists of short episodes sometimes only loosely connected with each other, the Passion is a fully developed story. The Passion brings to fulfilment our expectation, set up back in chapter nine, that Jesus would meet with suffering and death in Jerusalem. The story has laid a trail that leads the reader to expect such a result. As is so often the case in Luke's Gospel, though, the question for us readers is not so much 'what will happen?' but 'how will it happen?'

As we have just seen, chapters twenty and twenty-one immediately preceding the Passion only increase the tension: the chief priests and scribes have responded to Jesus' presence in Jerusalem with murderous intent but they seem unable to act while Jesus enjoys the support of the people in general. This in fact is the problem that the Passion sets up right at the outset: *how* can the leaders bring about their plan to dispose of Jesus in spite of the people? (22:2) The answer will eventually involve manipulating the Roman authorities. More immediately, however, the problem facing the leaders is a practical one: how to take Jesus into custody apart from the people's knowledge.

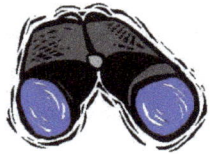

The first part of the Passion (22:1-53) is thus the story of how Jesus goes from being a free man in Jerusalem (with a protective circle of loyal disciples and the people) to being a lone prisoner of the Temple authorities, on trial for his life. This part of the Passion reads somewhat like a miniature spy-thriller. There are three main scenes in the drama. In the first (22:1-6), the problem is introduced and a solution proposed: Judas, one of the Twelve, secretly meets with the authorities and agrees to look for a way to hand Jesus over to them when no crowd is present.

The second scene focuses on the preparations for and celebration of Passover (22:7-38). With Judas seeking an

---

> THE FIRST PART OF THE PASSION (22:1-53) IS THUS THE STORY OF HOW JESUS GOES FROM BEING A FREE MAN IN JERUSALEM (WITH A PROTECTIVE CIRCLE OF LOYAL DISCIPLES AND THE PEOPLE) TO BEING A LONE PRISONER OF THE TEMPLE AUTHORITIES, ON TRIAL FOR HIS LIFE. THIS PART OF THE PASSION READS SOMEWHAT LIKE A MINIATURE SPY-THRILLER.

opportunity to alert the authorities to a moment when Jesus will be away from the protective barrier of the crowds, the preparations for the Passover meal take on a dangerous significance: if Judas knows in advance where Jesus will be on that night he can alert the authorities and hand him over while the people are otherwise occupied with their own Passover celebrations. It is therefore significant that Luke tells a story in which Jesus himself initiates preparations: contrast Mark where it is the disciples who do this (Mark 14:12). Luke implies that Jesus is well aware of the danger. It is not that Jesus wishes to avoid capture – in later going to the Mount of Olives, Jesus virtually puts himself into the hands of his enemies—but we will be told that this particular Passover is one which Jesus has 'eagerly desired' to eat with his apostles (22:15). Nothing can be allowed to disrupt the Passover meal itself and careful preparations are required to ensure that this occurs. To do this he engages two of the inner circle, Peter and John, to prepare the meal. In response to Jesus' direction to prepare the Passover, Peter and John ask a crucial question: 'where?'

WHERE TO GO FOR PASSOVER?

That these leading disciples have no idea where Jesus intends to celebrate Passover makes it clear that neither does Judas. The sense of secrecy is enhanced as Jesus refuses to name a place but gives Peter and John a sign: a man carrying a water jar inside the city gates whom they are to follow. They are also given a 'password' for the owner of the house, 'The teacher asks you…' (22:11) Luke leaves it deliciously ambiguous for the reader: are we are meant to understand Jesus as having prophetic knowledge or as the instigator of a counter-conspiracy against Judas? The unfolding of the preparations shows that Jesus remains in control of events beyond even the disciples' knowledge.

The tension increases as the people disappear from view and the traitor eats with the betrayed. This "last supper" of Jesus with his disciples provided the model for the gatherings of the early Christians and is the origin of the Eucharistic celebrations of Christians down to the present day. The word "Eucharist" itself is used by Luke to describe Jesus' thanksgiving over the bread and cups of wine (22:17, 19). This element of thanksgiving to God was considered so important that it eventually came to be a shorthand way of referring to the Lord's Supper as a whole. While all four New Testament accounts of the last supper include the word "eucharist", they differ in various ways (see Matt 26:26-29; Mark 14:22-25; 1 Cor 11:23-26). For example, only Luke mentions two cups of wine, one at the beginning and one at the end of the meal. While the Christian Eucharist today uses only a single cup, Luke's Gospel reflects the Passover practice, then and now, of several shared cups of wine.

Among the Gospels, only in Luke does Jesus explicitly ask his disciples to repeat the meal in remembrance of him. It is important to realise that the act of remembering was not simply thinking about something that happened in the past, but something that actually brought the reality and power of a past event to bear on the present. Celebrating the Passover meal enables participants to take their part in the events it commemorates. As such, an integral part of the Passover meal is the host's explanation or interpretation of the symbolic elements of the meal. For the people of Israel, then and now, the meal is interpreted in terms of God's great act of liberation on behalf of his people enslaved in Egypt. As host, Jesus now re-interprets the bread and cup in terms of the death he is about to undergo. His body will be given or handed over 'for' the participants in this meal; in other words, his death is not to be interpreted as meaningless defeat, but as in some way benefiting his disciples. What this benefit is will be further explained with the cup: Jesus' death will bring a 'new covenant' between God and humanity. And just as with the great covenant of the Old Testament (Exod 24:3-8), so blood is also the sign of this new covenant. Therefore, to celebrate the Eucharist in remembrance of Jesus is to share in the new relationship with God that his death mysteriously enables. At this highpoint of the meal, though, Jesus stuns the disciples by announcing that he is to be betrayed by one of them.

> ONLY LUKE REPORTS THAT A GREAT NUMBER OF THE PEOPLE FOLLOWED JESUS BEARING HIS CROSS, INCLUDING WOMEN MOURNING FOR HIM. PASSERS-BY DO NOT DERIDE JESUS IN LUKE'S ACCOUNT, BUT INSTEAD THE PEOPLE STAND THERE WATCHING SILENTLY

While the reader knows that Judas is the one, this remains a mystery to the disciples and they ask one another 'which one of them it could be who would do this' (22:23). That they all stand perilously close to the edge of betrayal is only too clear from the ensuing argument about who is the greatest among them. Here, in the last moments they will spend with their teacher before he goes to his death, the disciples have still failed to grasp the tremendous role-reversal which God's kingdom implies: the one who places himself or herself last and in the role of a servant is the one who is truly 'great' in the kingdom which Jesus inaugurates.

The third scene in the first act of the Passion (22:39-53) sees Jesus handed over into the power of the chief priests. He leaves the comparative safety of the crowded city where the disciples might have raised the alarm against any attempt to capture him and goes to the nearby Mount of Olives 'as was his custom'. There is no longer any concern for secrecy on Jesus' part; he has celebrated the Passover with his disciples and now all that remains is for him to go to the death which leads to his kingdom.

The arrest of Jesus, followed by Peter's denial, leads to a double trial: one before the council (or Sanhedrin) of elders, chief priests and scribes, the other before Pilate. The trial before the Sanhedrin involves an argument about two of the key titles given to Jesus prior to and at the time of his birth: 'Messiah' (2:11, 26) and 'Son of God' (1:35). To claim the title Messiah was not religiously offensive in itself; the reason that the Sanhedrin is interested in whether Jesus claims to be the Messiah lies in their intention to exploit the political ramifications of this before Pilate. On the other hand, the title 'Son of God' carries unmistakeable hints of blasphemy.

The sudden appearance of these titles in the Sanhedrin trial is rather unexpected since they rarely appear in the Gospel and Jesus never claims them for himself. In fact, early in his ministry, Jesus silences the demons who came out of people shouting 'You are the Son of God' and 'knew that he was the Messiah' (4:41). The only human character who explicitly acknowledges Jesus as Messiah is Peter (9:20). Luke's sparing and careful handling of these titles in his story perhaps indicates how explosive these titles really were. They are easily misunderstood, and when misunderstood, extremely dangerous.

DINNER AND A SHOW TRIAL

This is not meant to be a well-conducted legal proceeding: it should strike the reader for what it is: a 'show-trial'. As has been clear from the beginning of the Passion, the chief priests and their associates are less interested in finding an actual punishable offence than they are in finding a way to put to death a man whom they consider an illegitimate rival to their leadership. For them, the end justifies the means: the main problem for the chief priests is how to interest the Roman authorities in the case and thus put Jesus' fate beyond doubt.

The Roman authorities were generally tolerant of the differing religions and traditions of their subject peoples as long as taxes were paid and public order maintained. The chief priests attempt to press both these buttons with Pilate, claiming that Jesus is seditious as evidenced by his forbidding the payment of taxes and his claim that he is the Messiah, a king (23:2). The reader knows that neither charge is true. In fact, when the chief priests previously tried to entrap Jesus on a charge of encouraging the people not to pay Roman taxes, they failed miserably (20:20-26) with Jesus publicly stating, 'give to the emperor the things that are the emperor's'. The mere mention of taxes would get Pilate interested, but realising how shaky the charge was, they shift the emphasis to a charge that Jesus is a threat to public order by claiming a kingship not recognised by the Roman state.

As we have seen, Jesus never makes such a claim publicly, and evades the question as to whether he is the Messiah. There is, however, a basis for the charge: only a matter of days previously, on entering Jerusalem, Jesus has been acclaimed as 'the king who comes in the name of the Lord' (19:38). Pilate is asked to believe that this can only be the result of Jesus himself having made such a claim. Jesus' popularity among the people, once a protective shield around him, is now turned against him by the chief priests as the very evidence of his danger to public order.

For the first time since the beginning of the Passion, the people re-appear as Pilate calls together 'the chief priests, the leaders and the people' (23:13) to hear his verdict. While Mark and Matthew clearly involve the people or crowds – stirred up by their leaders – in the demand for Jesus' death, Luke remains extremely vague about who it is that actually demands the crucifixion of Jesus (23:18). Overall, Luke maintains the basically positive attitude of the people towards Jesus. Only Luke reports that a great number of the people followed Jesus bearing his cross, including women mourning for him. Passers-by do not deride Jesus in Luke's account, but instead the people stand there watching silently (23:35); only the leaders and soldiers are singled out by Luke as mockers.

Again, only in Luke are we told that the crowds returned home after Jesus' death beating their breasts: that is, in repentance and mourning (23:48). Luke's presentation of the people in the final part of the Passion is important for what will follow in Acts: the people gathered in Jerusalem are not implacably opposed to God's visitation in the person of Jesus. They did allow themselves, like the disciples, to be manipulated into fearful silence, but they remained with Jesus and witnessed the death of an innocent man. Their repentant mourning, like Peter's, allows for the possibility of a new relationship with the Risen Jesus that Peter will proclaim at Pentecost.

INNOCENT AND SENTENCED

26 As they led him away, they seized a man, Simon of Cyrene, who was coming from the country, and they laid the cross on him, and made him carry it behind Jesus. 27A great number of the people followed him, and among them were women who were beating their breasts and wailing for him. 28But Jesus turned to them and said, 'Daughters of Jerusalem, do not weep for me, but weep for yourselves and for your children. 29For the days are surely coming when they will say, "Blessed are the barren, and the wombs that never bore, and the breasts that never nursed." 30Then they will begin to say to the mountains, "Fall on us"; and to the hills, "Cover us." 31For if they do this when the wood is green, what will happen when it is dry?'

32 Two others also, who were criminals, were led away to be put to death with him. 33When they came to the place that is called The Skull, they crucified Jesus* there with the criminals, one on his right and one on his left. 34Then Jesus said, 'Father, forgive them; for they do not know what they are doing.' And they cast lots to divide his clothing. 35And the people stood by, watching; but the leaders scoffed at him, saying, 'He saved others; let him save himself if he is the Messiah of God, his chosen one!' 36The soldiers also mocked him, coming up and offering him sour wine, 37and saying, 'If you are the King of the Jews, save yourself!' 38There was also an inscription over him, 'This is the King of the Jews.'

39 One of the criminals who were hanged there kept deriding him and saying, 'Are you not the Messiah? Save yourself and us!' 40But the other rebuked him, saying, 'Do you not fear God, since you are under the same sentence of condemnation? 41And we indeed have been condemned justly, for we are getting what we deserve for our deeds, but this man has done nothing wrong.' 42Then he said, 'Jesus, remember me when you come into your kingdom.' 43He replied, 'Truly I tell you, today you will be with me in Paradise.'

44 It was now about noon, and darkness came over the whole land until three in the afternoon, 45while the sun's light failed; and the curtain of the temple was

---

LUKE REPORTS NO CRY OF DESOLATION FROM THE CROSS.
INSTEAD JESUS IS CONFIDENT OF HIS FATHER'S PRESENCE;
HE PRAYS FOR FORGIVENESS
FOR HIS PERSECUTORS
AND HANDS OVER HIS LIFE TO THE FATHER.

torn in two. 46Then Jesus, crying with a loud voice, said, 'Father, into your hands I commend my spirit.' Having said this, he breathed his last. 47When the centurion saw what had taken place, he praised God and said, 'Certainly this man was innocent.' 48And when all the crowds who had gathered there for this spectacle saw what had taken place, they returned home, beating their breasts. 49But all his acquaintances, including the women who had followed him from Galilee, stood at a distance, watching these things. (Luke 23: 26-49)

Luke's account of Jesus' death is distinctive. Of all the evangelists, Luke is the least interested in the physical abuse of Jesus; in fact it is quite striking how little Luke tells us compared with the others. In Gethsemane, Luke's description omits Mark's emphasis on Jesus' distress and grief; instead it is the disciples who sleep because of grief (22:45). While Jesus is said to be "in anguish" or "agony" (22:43), the Greek word *agonia* suggests the extreme exertion of an athlete striving for victory rather than mere pain. As such, he perspires so profusely that his sweat is *like* drops of blood falling to the ground. Luke tones down Mark's description of the abuse by the temple guards by omitting reference to their spitting on him (22:63-65). Mark's scene of the Roman soldiers' abuse with the crown of thorns and reed sceptre is omitted entirely by Luke: instead, Herod's soldiers merely put an elegant robe on Jesus and mock him (23:11). Instead of both of the condemned criminals taunting him, in Luke one actually seeks salvation from Jesus (23:42). Luke reports no cry of desolation from the cross. Instead Jesus is confident of his Father's presence; he prays for forgiveness for his persecutors and hands over his life to the Father.

Naturally, Luke is not denying the real suffering of Jesus. But Luke understands the significance of the Passion in a way that places the emphasis less on Jesus' suffering than on his free adherence to the Father's will. Luke also emphasises Jesus' consciousness of the Father's presence with him, and his constant concern in the midst of his own suffering for the weakness, sin and suffering of others: the women of Jerusalem, his crucifiers, the repentant criminal. As Luke understands it, concern for the weakness of sinful humanity is uppermost in Jesus' mind during his Passion, just as it has been throughout his ministry. This is not the bitter failure of all Jesus has said and done, but the highpoint and culmination of his ministry.

Resurrection (Luke 24)

EASTER SCENES
ARE WE THERE YET?

The climax of each of the gospels is the proclamation that the brutal death of Jesus is not the end of the story. Each of the gospels recounts that some female disciples (Mary Magdalene is the only one named in all four gospels) go to the tomb early in the morning after the Sabbath rest, but discover it to be empty and receive a message that Jesus has risen. It is a surprising fact that beyond these most basic elements, all four gospels differ in the details of what occurs at the tomb itself and in the immediate aftermath. For example, the evangelists differ on the identity of the messenger(s): an 'angel' (Matt 28:5), 'a young man dressed in a white robe' (Mark 16:5), 'two men in dazzling clothes' (Luke 24:4), 'two angels in white' (John 20:12).

The gospels, however, do not simply end with the Easter proclamation, 'He is Risen!' They also provide mysterious stories of encounter between the disciples and the risen Jesus himself; in this respect each gospel gives a unique perspective on the Easter experience of the disciples. Matthew, for example, tells of the meeting between disciples and Jesus on the mountain in Galilee where Jesus commissions them to 'go out to the whole world' (Matt 28:16-20). John gives us the stories of the appearances in the upper room with the handing over of the Holy Spirit and Thomas' coming to faith (John 20:19-29) and of the breakfast Jesus shares with his disciples on the shore of the Lake of Galilee (John 21:1-14). Luke's unique contribution to the early Christian traditions about Easter is his account of the two disciples who encounter the risen Jesus on the way to Emmaus.

Luke devotes an entire chapter to the resurrection and we need to read this chapter as a whole. Essentially, this story is about whether the disciples of Jesus will come to faith in the risen Jesus or whether they will remain at the point of knowing only Jesus' death. Can the disciples *see* what has really happened, and will they *respond* appropriately? Naturally, Luke expects that his readers, including us, will be challenged by these same questions as we come to the end of his Gospel.

The story begins as the women go to the tomb where they have seen the dead Jesus laid only hours before (24:1-3). The one absolute and certain fact that these women know is that they have seen Jesus killed and buried. Luke tells us that the women bring 'the spices they have prepared'. This is an important detail: they went equipped with the things they needed in order to deal with a corpse – there is not a shred of expectation in these disciples that the body of Jesus might be missing from the tomb, much less raised to life again. The tomb should be intact and the body should be there, but when they arrive they discover that it is not.

The aftermath of the death of Jesus is no longer straightforwardly self-evident. Of course, the empty tomb is not a sign of resurrection in itself. An empty tomb invites many natural explanations: the women have made a mistake and gone to the wrong grave; the body has

---

THE GOSPELS, HOWEVER, DO NOT SIMPLY END WITH THE EASTER PROCLAMATION, 'HE IS RISEN!' THEY ALSO PROVIDE MYSTERIOUS STORIES OF ENCOUNTER BETWEEN THE DISCIPLES AND THE RISEN JESUS HIMSELF; IN THIS RESPECT EACH GOSPEL GIVES A UNIQUE PERSPECTIVE ON THE EASTER EXPERIENCE OF THE DISCIPLES.

been stolen; the body has been moved, etc. The women are naturally perplexed. The possibility of belief in resurrection is not raised by the women but by 'two men in dazzling clothes': 'why look for the living among the dead?' (24:5) The message is delivered in a tone of mock disbelief, as if nothing could be more obvious than the resurrection! The women now 'remember' Jesus' words about rising from the dead, but it is not yet clear that they 'believe'. Certainly none of the other disciples pay any credence to their story of a vision (24:11), and although Peter goes to investigate, he remains simply 'amazed' (24:12).

ON THE ROAD TO EMMAUS

The Walk to Emmaus

13 Now on that same day two of them were going to a village called Emmaus, about seven miles* from Jerusalem, 14and talking with each other about all these things that had happened. 15While they were talking and discussing, Jesus himself came near and went with them, 16but their eyes were kept from recognizing him. 17And he said to them, 'What are you discussing with each other while you walk along?' They stood still, looking sad. 18Then one of them, whose name was Cleopas, answered him, 'Are you the only stranger in Jerusalem who does not know the things that have taken place there in these days?' 19He asked them, 'What things?' They replied, 'The things about Jesus of Nazareth, who was a prophet mighty in deed and word before God and all the people, 20and how our chief priests and leaders handed him over to be condemned to death and crucified him. 21But we had hoped that he was the one to redeem Israel. Yes, and besides all this, it is now the third day since these things took place. 22Moreover, some women of our group astounded us. They were at the tomb early this morning, 23and when they did not find his body there, they came back and told us that they had indeed seen a vision of angels who said that he was alive. 24Some of those who were with us went to the tomb and found it just as the women had said; but they did not see him.' 25Then he said to them, 'Oh, how foolish you are, and how slow of heart to believe all that the prophets have declared! 26Was it not necessary that the Messiah should suffer these things and then enter into his glory?' 27Then beginning with Moses and all the prophets, he interpreted to them the things about himself in all the scriptures.

28As they came near the village to which they were going, he walked ahead as if he were going on. 29But they urged him strongly, saying, 'Stay with us, because it is almost evening and the day is now nearly over.' So he went in to stay with them. 30When he was at the table with them, he took bread, blessed and broke it, and gave it to them. 31Then their eyes were opened, and they recognized him; and he vanished from their sight. 32They said to each other, 'Were not our hearts burning within us while he was talking to us on the road, while he was opening the scriptures to us?' 33That same hour they got up and returned to Jerusalem; and they found the eleven and their companions gathered together. 34They were saying, 'The Lord has risen indeed, and he has appeared to Simon!' 35Then they told what had happened on the road, and how he had been made known to them in the breaking of the bread. (Luke 24:13-35)

In light of what has occurred at the tomb, the Emmaus story (24:13-49) shows disciples moving from the possibility of belief in the resurrection to its realisation. So far, Jesus has been proclaimed as risen, but he himself has not been recognised as such by anyone. Now two disciples recognise Jesus as present with them and return to Jerusalem to evangelise the others.

Luke marks these two disciples out from the group of 'the eleven and all the rest' to whom the women bring news of the empty tomb and the vision of heavenly messengers. It is clear that they are as yet unbelievers in the resurrection (24:11) even though they are aware of the latest news from the tomb. The two disciples are moving away from Jerusalem. They are moving away from the epicentre of the narrative, hopeless and despondent. They have separated themselves from the community of disciples.

The journey theme is clearly important here, as it was in the travel narrative. The first appearance of the risen Jesus in Luke's Gospel takes place 'on the way: in a sense, this is the travel narrative in miniature. Just as Jesus spent the journey towards Jerusalem trying to teach his disciples about the reality and meaning of his suffering, death and resurrection, now he does the same on a journey *away* from Jerusalem. Now by contrast however, the disciples are receptive: instead of misunderstanding and hardness of heart, these disciples experience their hearts burning within them (24:32).

While the disciples converse about the events in Jerusalem, the meaning of those events is not self-evident. Not even the death of Jesus is simply a fact to be accepted; the empty tomb has complicated that, not to mention the women's story about heavenly messengers. Ironically, while they dismissed the words of the women as an 'idle tale', these two are now engaged in idle chatter themselves: they *literally* don't know what they're talking about!

Luke uses a classic story-telling technique here by letting the reader in on a secret, giving us information that the characters don't have: we know that it's Jesus who is walking alongside, but the two disciples don't. The effect is to interest us in whether and how the characters will come to this knowledge. Failure to recognise the risen Jesus is a theme that recurs in various ways in the different gospels. This might seem to us to be a rather embarrassing fact: how could Jesus' closest followers not recognise him? Our embarrassment was clearly not shared by the evangelists who chose to include these stories in their gospels. Part of the reason they did so was surely that they realised that the resurrection of Jesus was something altogether unique and not something which could be perceived purely and simply by the naked eye, but by eyes aided by faith.

The conversation between the unrecognised Jesus and the disciples is filled with as much tragic irony as any episode in the New Testament. The one who is repeatedly shown to know the interior thoughts of others, asks in an innocent tone 'What are you discussing?' (24:17) In exquisite detail, Luke stops the movement that otherwise characterises this story and gives us a rare description of the appearance of his characters: they are sad – indeed the Greek word used here might be translated as 'gloomy' – there is a sense of resignation about their sadness, and it shows. A disciple named Cleopas answers (24:18), 'Are you the only stranger in Jerusalem who does not know the things that have taken place there in these days?'

TALKING TO A STRANGER

Not only do they not recognise Jesus, but as if to hammer the point home that they haven't got a clue, they actually see him as a 'stranger'. Of course, far from being the only one who does *not* know the things that have happened in Jerusalem, this 'stranger' is in fact the only one who really *does* know! The refer-

> LUKE USES A CLASSIC STORY-TELLING TECHNIQUE HERE BY LETTING THE READER IN ON A SECRET, GIVING US INFORMATION THAT THE CHARACTERS DON'T HAVE: WE KNOW THAT IT'S JESUS WHO IS WALKING ALONGSIDE, BUT THE TWO DISCIPLES DON'T. THE EFFECT IS TO INTEREST US IN WHETHER AND HOW THE CHARACTERS WILL COME TO THIS KNOWLEDGE.

ence to 'these days' implies the events of the passion and death of Jesus, but the disciples' fixation on these days blinds them from the greater perspective that might help them to understand these events. Jesus will help them to see these days in the light of all the scriptures and thus to know their significance.

Following Jesus' question the disciples tell their story in the form of a kind of tiny summary of the gospel so far. They begin to move in the direction of understanding even as they relate their story: the things involve not just a man named Jesus, but a man whose career showed him to be a prophet mighty in deed and word before God and all the people. The fact that the disciples even get this far is a hopeful sign. Like the women, they have begun the process of remembering. For the disciples, attention focuses on the mismatch between Jesus' identity as a prophet and his death at the hands of the leaders in Jerusalem. In this sense, they are both near to the truth but also still far from it: they can't make the connection.

The story so far, drawing on Israel's wider story, makes it clear that this is precisely the kind of fate that awaits prophets in Israel. Their hope that Jesus might be the one to redeem Israel has faded because they cannot see how the death of the prophet might itself form part of God's redemptive plan. Similarly, they can make no sense of the empty tomb. However, what they first thought of as an 'idle tale' told by the women has apparently been working on their minds in light of the fact that some of their companions were at least able to verify the women's story that the tomb was empty. So now they describe themselves as astounded, and relate part of the women's tale to this stranger.

> DESPITE HIS DISCIPLES' TEMPTATIONS TO SLIP BACK INTO FEAR AND DENIAL OF THE RESURRECTION, JESUS RE-ASSURES THEM THAT HE IS RISEN BODILY AND OPENS THEIR MINDS TO FULL UNDERSTANDING.

They have begun to reflect rather than merely to dismiss. They come so close to understanding: they even tell the stranger that this is the 'third day' – exactly as Jesus himself had prophesied—and yet they fail to grasp the significance. They have all the raw materials available to them for making sense of recent events but they are as yet unable to make a correct interpretation.

The stranger, whom the disciples have treated, literally, as 'ignorant', now takes charge of the conversation in a startling way. He accuses them of being 'foolish' and so reflects the exasperation that we feel by this point at the inability of these disciples to put the pieces together. The stranger is not ignorant – *they* are! The central question is: 'was it not necessary that the Messiah should suffer these things and then enter into his glory?' (24:26). It is Jesus who introduces the term 'Messiah' for the first time: in so doing he identifies this 'prophet' that they have been discussing with the Messiah.

We might wonder why the disciples do not even mention this aspect of Jesus' identity. It was bad enough for these disciples that a prophet should die in such a way; it was unthinkable, unspeakable, that the Messiah should be crucified. Jesus thus pushes the disciples to the boundaries of what is possible for them even to imagine. Luke makes it clear that Jesus *interprets* the scriptures, beginning with Moses and the prophets. While Luke does not give us the content of Jesus' teaching here, it is implied that the link is made at the level of the prophetic character of the Messiah: prophets were anointed, prophets were expected to face a career marked by suffering and rejection. Could it not be that the chief anointed one, the Messiah, might also share in the fate of the prophets?

Another dramatic moment arrives as the destination draws near. Jesus actually walks ahead; he has already begun to leave them, and they still remain ignorant. Now the disciples must make the next move and take the initiative. We will discover shortly that they have been having a strange experience while Jesus has been talking: their hearts have been burning. And so they urge Jesus not to go on, but to stay with them. They offer hospitality to Jesus – no small thing in a gospel where meals have been so important as signs of the kingdom of God. Once at table, however, Jesus again takes charge; taking, blessing, breaking, and giving bread. While there is some allusion here to the feeding of the 5000 (9:16), we will naturally connect these actions to those of the Last Supper and thus to the Eucharist. In any case, the breaking of bread finally reveals the presence of the risen Jesus to his disciples.

What happens next parallels the conditions at the beginning of the story, but in reverse. In contrast to their eyes being 'held', they are now 'opened'; they recognise him now, but in contrast to drawing near them, he vanishes. The disciples once again converse with each other, now not about the events in Jerusalem, but about their experience on the road and they identify the importance of the opening of the scriptures as crucial for their coming to this moment of insight. Hearts that were slow have begun to burn.

RETURN JOURNEY

Luke impresses upon us the urgency of sharing their recognition of the risen Jesus with the others. The journey away from Jerusalem was told in great detail, as if to mirror the slowness of hearts and the gloominess of the disciples. Now, they are up in an instant and back to Jerusalem! There, they find their companions all abuzz; while they have been on the road, Jesus has appeared to Simon. The disciples refer to Jesus as 'Lord', a title implying faith.

It is not just that God has raised Jesus from the dead, but that they now understand that Jesus is the one through whom the gracious presence of God will continue to be present to them. The two disciples give their report of what happened on the road and how Jesus had been made known in the breaking of the bread. Interpretation of the scriptures and the breaking of bread go together just as they will in the early church in (Acts 2:42).

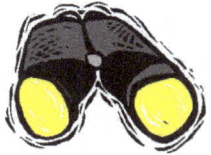

The gospel concludes with one final appearance of the risen Jesus to the assembled disciples (24:36-53); above all, it's in the community of disciples that Jesus will be encountered. Despite his disciples' temptations to slip back into fear and denial of the resurrection, Jesus reassures them that he is risen bodily and opens their minds to full understanding, including the announcement of their missionary role. His own mission complete, Jesus now completes his exodus to the Father, leaving the disciples where the gospel story began, in the Jerusalem Temple praising God. The story has come full circle, but we are not simply 'back to square one.' There has been a dramatic change brought about in this story, since the people praising God in the temple are now those who have resurrection faith. It is this faith, confirmed with the promised gift of the Risen One's Holy Spirit, that allows the Lukan narrative to spring forward into the story of Acts.

In the Gospel according to Luke we gain an insight into the beliefs of the first Christians about Jesus of Nazareth. For Luke and his first readers, Jesus was the Messiah and Son of God whose words and actions spoke powerfully of the liberating and inclusive power of the kingdom of God. However, this Gospel is more than just a window into ancient history. Luke has created a story that continues to speak to readers across the ages. In a world that still longs for peace and justice, Luke's message about the God who cares especially for those who are most vulnerable remains a source of inspiration and hope.

www.ingramcontent.com/pod-product-compliance
Lightning Source LLC
Chambersburg PA
CBHW061059170426
43199CB00025B/2941